INSIGHTS
INTO THE
MYSTERY
OF THE
TRINITY

Second Edition

AUSTIN DE BOURG

Unless otherwise noted, all Scriptures are taken from the King James Version of the Bible.

ISBN: 1491289880
ISBN-13: 9781491289884

Library of Congress Control Number: 2013914635
CreateSpace Independent Publishing Platform
North Charleston, South Carolina

DEDICATION

This book is dedicated to
the Trinity,
Who live in my heart
and I in Theirs,
And Whose Spirit allows me
to know the secret things
that pertain to Them.

ACKNOWLEDGEMENT

I wish to acknowledge Althea Bastien, Maria Parris, and Toni Kimbrough for their labor of love in searching through the manuscript for any type of errors they could find; for drilling me on structure and points they thought needed clarification and deeper expression; for typing and retyping. Together, through their godly maturity and analytical minds, they proved to be invaluable contributors to the final product.

I also acknowledge Michaella Frederick, whose proofreading and copy editing aided in the preparation of the final manuscript.

It deals with
questions we dare to ask
and
answers we dare to give.

- How could Jesus Christ be God and man at the same time? Can this be affirmed?

- Why would the Almighty God need a Son and a Holy Spirit? Is He lacking in Himself?

- Why would such a good and perfect God make such a bad devil?

- How was Lucifer, now known as Satan, able to sin and corrupt himself in such a pure and holy environment as heaven?

- Why would God cast Satan out of heaven to earth where He has two innocent children? Why didn't God intervene on their behalf?

- Why would Adam and Eve, who had God's warning not to eat from the Tree of Knowledge of Good and Evil, do so nevertheless?

and more . . .

ENDORSEMENTS

The book *Insights into the Mystery of the Trinity* by Pastor Austin de Bourg provides welcome enlightenment on fundamental matters such as creation, God's purpose for man, and how Satan came into being with his malevolence. It gives a graphic account of the battle between Christ and Satan, and the victory of Christ over the devil in his stolen domain.

Its title *Insights into the Mystery of the Trinity* is an explicit introduction to the book's contents.

I met Pastor de Bourg through a member of his Church. I was so impressed by her knowledge of the scripture and by her way of life that I asked to meet her Pastor. She introduced me to Pastor de Bourg. I heard him deliver his message on several occasions and, on each occasion, left with the desire to hear more. His is a teaching ministry. This book is an example of what he imparts.

Many will read this book, not only for knowledge but for spiritual development. Pastor de Bourg's declarations, interpretations and conclusions are supported by Biblical references.

—Hon. Arthur N. R. Robinson, T.C., O.C.C., S.C.
July 2006
Former President of the Republic of Trinidad & Tobago 1997–2003
Former Prime Minister of the Republic of Trinidad & Tobago 1986–1991

The time could not be more ripe than it is at this moment for a book such as *Insights into the Mystery of the Trinity*, authored by Austin J. de Bourg. There is a great necessity for this fundamental doctrine of the faith to find its place within the hearts of the people once again. Too many Christians accept the Trinity without any real, coherent understanding of why they believe in the Trinity. It is refreshing to be able to find, among the clutter of "exotic" literature that only titillates one's imagination, a book that solidifies the foundation of the faith which is the true essential for building a lasting, maturing relationship with God.

—Reverend Kelvin Siewdass

Contents

FOREWORD

God gives us a unique classic in this book authored by Austin J. de Bourg, *Insights into the Mystery of the Trinity*. Only someone who has been through the crucible, who has embraced the cross, and who has responded to God in the way that Austin de Bourg has done, could reach that level of intimacy with the Father, the Lord Jesus, and the Holy Spirit. They have entrusted Austin de Bourg with profound revelation and insights into the mystery of all mysteries—the mystery of the Trinity.

This book goes far beyond one's greatest expectations as it provides the answers to questions no one previously dared to answer about God and His dealings with mankind. The author explains, from God's standpoint, why God does things the way He does, contrary to our own reasoning, and clarifies controversial issues surrounding God, Jesus Christ, and Christianity.

Do yourself a favor and read this book with an open mind and allow it to transport you to the spiritual dimension where God exists. As you read, you will begin to contemplate God in His omniscience and omnipotence. You will realize just how much mankind has reduced and limited God to the senses in an attempt to humanize this supernatural, infinite God. When we view God this way, we make Him familiar and ordinary. This is a book to wake us up and cause us to understand the great plans that God has for mankind. I guarantee you that, by the end of this book, you will have a clearer understanding of your own purpose, as well as a more expanded perspective of the Trinity, of Jesus Christ, and of Christianity.

For me, the experience of reading this book brought light and understanding of the purpose and administration of the Trinity, resulting in a renewal of thought and spirit. I have a much deeper understanding now of the Trinity's collaborative mission to restore man's relationship, fellowship and dialogue with God. As an added bonus, while journeying through the pages of this insightful work, I found along the way many other mysteries revealed that had remained hidden until now.

This book is a treatise validating the Trinity, Jesus Christ, and the supernatural nature and heritage of Christianity. It takes you where no one has gone before, to see beyond human limits and explores the secret things of God which He delights to reveal. It is a treasure-house of precious insights and revelation. It ventures into eternity and follows God from His first creative expression, at the conception of the Trinity, then to the creation of the heavens and the earth, and onto His greatest creation—man—in whom God placed His image and likeness. This simple, well-written, well-constructed book is full of priceless gems waiting to be collected as it spans from eternity to Pentecost, and beyond.

It helped me sift through the confusion of conflicting doctrinal, philosophical and intellectual dogma and focus once again on the truth of God—who He is, who I am in Him, and what my purpose is in the midst of the noise and confusion. The spiritual corruption and pollution, the hustle of daily living so quickly erases God from the mind and heart.

This book belongs in every library, seminary, Bible school, secular school, church, and home. It maintains and preserves the truth and dignity of God and teaches us to love God, to fear God, to honor God, to love our neighbor as we love ourselves, and to fulfill God's purpose.

—Toni Deborah Kimbrough

Author's Preface

The book *Insights into the Mystery of the Trinity* does not claim to contain complete knowledge and understanding of the subject of the Trinity. It does claim, however, to give in-depth insights into the reason and purpose for, and the administration of, the Trinity of God, and explains the necessity and heightened relevance of such insights in these times.

The Trinity is not a mystery to the angels and the saints in the celestial Kingdom of God where knowledge is superior and they have ready access to God, Who is the source of knowledge. It is a mystery, however, in the terrestrial realm where knowledge is limited and we do not have ready access to God. It has always been God's intention, though, to impart to us as much knowledge as we are able to contain, both of the terrestrial and celestial realms, in order for us to shape our thinking and to pattern our lives to that of heaven.

Many consider the mystery of the Trinity to be the mystery of all mysteries. There is, however, a mindset about the word 'mystery' that seems to indicate that mysteries are too difficult or impossible to understand. With that way of thinking, one could read the explanation of a revealed mystery and struggle to understand it. When a mystery is unveiled, it is no longer a mystery, yet, in the minds of those with this pattern of thinking, a mystery is a mystery and would always be a mystery. That mindset is often a hindrance to receiving the revelation of a mystery.

As you read this book with the correct approach to the things of God, you would have no difficulty grasping the mystery of the Trinity as it unfolds in the chapters.

Insights into the Mystery of the Trinity spans from eternity to Pentecost and beyond. It includes the noble and honorable role of the Jewish nation out of which Christ came, Christianity emerged, and God and man reconciled.

While writing this book, I received insights from God which have shed light on other mysteries and perplexing questions which I have also shared throughout the book.

Insights into the Mystery of the Trinity gives a closer and more personal glimpse of God-Omnipotence-Omniscience. As you read it, I pray for a sharpening of your vision and understanding of His purpose for all mankind and, finally, I pray that it will bring you into an intimate relationship with the Trinity.

In eternity, God's lone existence was purposeless,
unproductive, and meaningless. God—Omnipotence—
purposed two extensions of Himself:
His own Word and His own Spirit.

One God—Three Persons.

Now, Omnipotence has dimension, meaning, and purpose.
The Father spoke, His Word affirmed it,
His Spirit brought it to pass.

"Let Us make man in Our image, after Our likeness . . ."

The Father, the Word and the Spirit, being one and
the same, existed in eternity. When the Word became
flesh on earth,
the Father gave Him an earthly name,
Emmanuel, meaning God with us—Jesus!

The Trinity is the three Persons of God,
each distinct yet One; united in purpose and function
as They restore man's relationship to God.

The Trinity had to step forward to do what only
They can do out of Their love for mankind.

INTRODUCTION

Why Mysteries?

The sovereignty of God is undeniable. Coupled with His omniscience, the right remains His to divulge plans for mankind and the entire universe as He wills. His actions are always guided by plan, purpose, and objective. Some of His purposes, plans, and truths remain hidden in Him and though we may witness and experience the evidence of these truths, we do not comprehend them. Their revelation remains veiled from our natural understanding. It is not that God does not want us to understand His mysteries, but He unveils them, as He deems necessary, at specific times, according to His plan and for His purpose.

> The secret things belong unto the LORD our God: but those
> things which are revealed belong unto us and to our children
> for ever, that we may do all the words of this law.
> —Deuteronomy 29:29

The Apostle Paul, speaking of his mission to the Gentiles, confirms in the book of Ephesians that it is only by divine revelation that such mysteries are understood. God unveils them as He wills, in His chosen time, and through whom He may choose—usually through His apostles and prophets.

> For this cause I Paul, the prisoner of Jesus Christ for you
> Gentiles,[2] If ye have heard of the dispensation of the grace of
> God which is given me to you-ward:[3] How that by revelation
> he made known unto me the mystery; (as I wrote afore in few

words,[4] Whereby, when ye read, ye may understand my knowledge in the mystery of Christ)[5] Which in other ages was not made known unto the sons of men, as it is now revealed unto his holy apostles and prophets by the Spirit;

—Ephesians 3:1–5

Paul draws upon his very own experiences in God and concludes that, indeed, one cannot figure out with one's natural ability and understanding the mysteries of God because they are kept in Him and revealed only by the Spirit of God when He wills.

As an example, Paul writes concerning the Gentiles, that there was a time when the Jews thought that they were the only ones who belonged to and therefore had access to God. The Gentiles had no place—so they thought—and that is why they looked down on them, referring to them as dogs and outcasts. In God's time however, having called Paul, He unveiled one of His mysteries to him: that there is a set time appointed by Him for the Gentiles to come in and to be a part of the same kingdom of which the Jews are a part—the time appointed to them, by God, to also be heirs of God.

The unveiling of this mystery doubtlessly shattered the assumptions held by the Jews about the Gentiles of that day. For those who received it, this revelation had positive, life-changing effects. Paul, having received it, was so impacted that it revolutionized his thinking and beliefs. With this new-found knowledge, Paul was now poised to take this truth to the Gentiles, thereby opening the door for them to come into the Kingdom of God. Had God continued to conceal this mystery, all, including the great Apostle Paul, would have maintained their thinking and perceptions about the Gentiles no matter how erroneous they were. We see, therefore, the importance and necessity of the unveiling of God's mysteries.

Mysteries, that are hidden truths, are in themselves the wisdom of God. God has veiled these truths from our understanding and unveils them at certain periods of time when learned men—the wise and the prudent, the genius, the philosopher, and the religious know-it-all—think that they have figured God out; when they presume to know how He thinks and acts; when they have become complacent toward God; when God becomes ordinary and familiar to them. It is usually at this point in time that God unveils one of His mysteries or hidden truths.

This revealed truth, when embraced by the believer, causes a revival of spirit and soul and a new appreciation and love for God and for His Word. It sets aflame man's determination to forge ahead to proclaim God in this new revealed light. When another generation or two have passed and this revealed truth becomes ordinary and familiar, complacency sets in again and men begin to treat God with irreverence and disregard. It is again time for God to unveil another mystery and a new revival begins in the spirit of man. God, knowing the heart of fallen man, is too wise to make known all His truths at once. Were He to do so, what recourse would He have to revive man's faith, love, obedience, affection, and devotion toward Him? If you study the history of the Church, you would see that world revivals were ignited and spread far and wide when the Spirit revealed a mystery that was hidden in His Word at a time when the heart of man had grown cold towards God.

The doctrine of the Trinity is one such mystery. In our time, God has chosen to unveil it for the benefit of those who have faithfully embraced it, though without comprehension. The unfolding of this mystery is also purposed to testify to the rest of the world, who have frowned at the idea of the Trinity, that God is infallible, and His Person, His Ways, and His Word can only be known by divine revelation and made known only by His Spirit.

The mystery of the Trinity has always been a challenge to the senses and intellect and has stirred much controversy by many varying thoughts. I expect, therefore, that readers would approach this book with a high degree of curiosity, seeking the answers concerning the Trinity of God. I must inform you, however, that the answers span from eternity to Pentecost and extend to the present time. In order to do justice to this topic, it was necessary along the way to unveil other mysteries and as I do, I will lay out the scriptural foundations for each mystery revealed. These mysteries and foundations are all relevant to this mystery of all mysteries—the mystery of the Trinity.

As you take this journey, you will find hidden treasures and you will be wiser and spiritually richer at the end.

CHAPTER I

THE CONCEPTION OF THE TRINITY

God is SUPREME. As such, there cannot be another with the title 'God' and nothing can equal or compare to God. If this were not so then God would not be God. He would not be Supreme. Within God are unlimited power, matchless wisdom, absolute knowledge, and ultimate creativity.

In eternity before time, God existed alone. Being alone is purposeless, unproductive, and meaningless. There existed no one with whom God could communicate and, therefore, He had no reason to express His characteristics and His creativity. He therefore purposed to initiate extensions of Himself, His own Word and His own Spirit. His existence would now have dimension, meaning and purpose. God would now release the creativity that is within Him and by so doing, give meaningful and purposeful expression to His existence. This He did!

God is a triune being—The Father, the First Person; the Word, the Second Person; and The Holy Spirit, the Third Person in The Trinity—and these three are One: one God but three persons or personalities, each distinct within Him yet one in purpose and function.

" If man would consider his own triune existence
of spirit, soul and body, he would cease to
question the Trinity of God. "

Their first creation was heaven and earth. God, The First Person, said, "Let there be light"; His Word, The Second Person, brought it into existence—light appeared; and His Spirit, The Third Person, gave it energy to function as God intended. God continued to declare, "Let there be . . . Let there be . . . Let there be . . ." and His Word brought it all into existence and His Spirit infused His creative energy over that which now existed, causing it to function. And so it was. All was created by His Word—things visible, and invisible; things celestial and terrestrial; things eternal and temporal. Earth's void, this dimensionless expanse was transformed by Omniscience and Omnipotence—God, The SUPREME who possesses no boundaries, no limits, and no impossibilities. That is Their state, Their position and Their right. Everything is created by Them and therefore subject to Them.

> In the beginning God created the heaven and the earth.[2] And the earth was without form, and void; and darkness was upon the face of the deep. And the Spirit of God moved upon the face of the waters.[3] And God said, Let there be light: and there was light.
>
> —Genesis 1:1–3

God chose the Apostle John to give the revelation of the conception of the Trinity, and John started the writing of his gospel with this revelation. John undoubtedly understood the importance and significance of this unique manifestation of God and that it would convey to mankind the reality and limitless ability and creativity of Omnipotence.

> In the beginning was the Word, and the Word was with God, and the Word was God.[2] The same was in the beginning with God.[3] All things were made by him; and without him was not any thing made that was made.[4] In him was life; and the life was the light of men.
>
> —John 1:1–4

This novel and superior concept of three persons in one God has always baffled man because it does not mathematically compute with the natural order of man's knowledge and, thus, has become a mystery to man. I believe, however, if man would consider his own triune existence of spirit, soul and body, he would cease to question the Trinity of God Who is all-mighty. Just as an individual's spoken word is a representation or reflection of that person, so too, a person's spirit is a representation or reflection of that person. In the case of God, He gave His voice and His Spirit distinct personalities to function as individuals apart from Him. His voice is the Word of God, expressed through Jesus Christ, in communicating with man on his human level and ultimately restoring mankind to God.

3

CHAPTER 2

GOD'S INTENTIONS FOR MAN

When God created man, it was for the purpose of sonship, relationship, communion, fellowship, and dialogue. That is why He made man in His image and likeness. Dialogue between God and man can only take place on a spiritual level. God is spirit and man has a spirit. Angels are the other created beings that share God's image and likeness, and are able to have communion, fellowship, and dialogue with God, irrespective of distance.

God did not speak man into being as He did with the rest of creation. He said to the Trinity, "Let Us make man in Our image, after Our likeness." Angels and man are God's greatest creation, His greatest works of art. God said that man is the apple of His eye. This means that God looks upon man with admiration as His creative masterpiece and values him above His other creations. God puts His creative ability within man and makes him a triune being of spirit, soul, and body. Man is created to be a reflection of God Himself, through His image and likeness in him.

As if to give visible expression and form to that which He conceived in its totality, God took the clay of the earth and meticulously shaped the figure of man and all his internals with His very own hands. The lifeless physical form lay before Him on completion, and He was satisfied that all was in place according to His unique design. God then breathed into it His very Spirit, giving it life.

> And the LORD God formed man of the dust of the ground, and breathed into his nostrils the breath of life; and man became a living soul.
>
> —Genesis 2:7

Earth was to be man's domain, so God formed his body from the earth and placed within him, a soul—the seat of his intellect, emotions, and will. The Spirit of God made the physical, natural man live. According to the Word of God, the Spirit gives life (John 6:63), therefore the image and likeness of God in Adam was in his spirit, not in his physical being. Man's spirit, then, is his dominant personality, having the greater influence over his soul and his body.

By design, God planted the Garden of Eden, and placed Adam and Eve in the Garden of Eden to dress it and to keep it. The Garden of Eden was a replica of heaven's paradise. Some of the same trees that are in heaven's paradise were in the Garden of Eden, including the Tree of Life. The waters of the river that ran through the garden were clear as crystal, as is the River of Life in heaven's paradise. The landscape was magnificent. On the surface of the earth, gold, diamond, and precious stones glistened in the sun, reflecting brilliant and colorful rays of light. Everything was right and perfect and God would come to the garden in the cool of the day to visit and have fellowship with Adam and Eve, His earthly children. They could not go to Him, limited by their earthly bodies, but He could come to them, unlimited because He is Spirit.

The communion between God and Adam and Eve was not flesh-to-flesh but it was Spirit-to-spirit because God is a Spirit and Adam's dominant personality was his spirit. There was no struggle or effort for Adam and God to talk to each other in the spirit. Natural words are not needed in this realm.

God gave Adam power, authority, and dominion over the earth and the right to name all the animals, birds, and every other created being, and God accepted the names that Adam gave them, because everything on the earth was under Adam's dominion, influence, and authority. This dominion and authority was his birthright. Everything on the earth was subject to him—yes, even the most powerful beasts of the earth. Likewise, Adam had dominion over the elements. He could regulate the wind and the waves of the sea if they became turbulent and he needed to calm them. Further, the image of God in Adam enabled him to be highly imaginative and creative like God, his Father. The widely accepted theory of evolution, which states that man evolved from apes, holds little credence if we consider the simple truth that children resemble their parents.

How then can a non-creative ape evolve into a highly creative being like a human? And why would God say He made man in His image and likeness? The name 'Adam' means first-born of its kind, unique, original.

Let me take a moment to verify through the scriptures my claim that Adam had authority over the animals, the wind, and the waves. The Bible informs us that Jesus Christ was the second Adam.

> And so it is written, The first man Adam was made a living soul; the last Adam was made a quickening spirit.[46] Howbeit that was not first which is spiritual, but that which is natural; and after- ward that which is spiritual.[47] The first man is of the earth, earthy: the second man is the Lord from heaven.[48] As is the earthy, such are they also that are earthy: and as is the heavenly, such are they also that are heavenly.[49] And as we have borne the image of the earthy, we shall also bear the image of the heavenly.[50] Now this I say, brethren, that flesh and blood cannot inherit the kingdom of God;
>
> —1 Corinthians 15:45–50a

Jesus Christ came as a perfect substitute for Adam, therefore, all the authority and power we see displayed through Jesus Christ was also resident in Adam.

See Jesus soundly asleep in the boat on the Sea of Galilee as the tempest rages all around. He rests in His spiritual birthright and in the superiority of His spiritual heritage and its inherent authority over the natural realm, and so He sleeps. Responding to the summons from His disciples, Jesus arises and speaks firmly and deliberately to the furious winds, "Peace be still," and immediately the winds and the waves were still.

On this occasion, Jesus was operating in the authority vested in Him through His spiritual birthright. Adam had the same spiritual birthright as Jesus but his disobedience to God robbed Adam of this dimension of power and authority.

Understand that we, Adam's offspring, were the intended heirs of his spiritual birthright. Because of this loss, the disciples of Jesus, also Adam's offspring, responded to the stormy seas with fear and desperation, obviously unable to exercise authority over the boisterous winds and the turbulent waters.

Our restoration, therefore, is not complete until we regain our spiritual birthright wherein we can exercise dominion and authority over the earth as God has ordained it. This will happen when sons of God step fully into resurrection life, the rebirth and resurgence of that spiritual dimension that Jesus Christ, the second Adam, has so graciously provided through His finished work on the cross.

FREE TO CHOOSE

God is Love and His perfection renders His love perfect and pure.

Placed within every human being is an inherent characteristic of life, to respond to his Maker. As with a child and his own parents, there is an inherent bonding within every child to his own mother and father, and, instinctively, the child does not yield its total confidence and trust to a stranger.

It is also fact that our free will is a part of life's inherent characteristic. Any violation of one's free will is therefore contrary to God's law, will, order, and plan for man. Satan, knowing this, set about to gain control of Adam and Eve's will by getting them to think that he was more concerned about them than God was. In their innocence, they did not know that Satan was the originator of lies, deception, and evil.

God is Love and His perfection renders His love perfect and pure. Because God made Adam in His image, this love of God was intrinsic to Adam and Eve's being. Therefore, God did not have to reveal Satan's deceptive powers to them because this intrinsic love, together with faith and obedience to Him as their Father and God, were quite sufficient to cause them to respond appropriately to anything or anyone who contradicted God's command. Not to express love, faith and obedience to God would be contrary to that which was inherent. This love for God must come from a voluntary expression of faith and obedience, demonstrated in purity of heart, mind, and action. Any other response is impure and God cannot receive it because of His perfect nature and character. For Adam and Eve in their original state, and for the true children of God who are born again with the restored image and nature of God, it is possible to love as God loves and this love is expressed through faith and obedience to His Word. The fallen man, however, finds it impossible to love as God loves.

Since the fall of man, his sinful nature has expressed love out of convenience, fear, and, sometimes, out of force. This does not constitute love as God created it to be, and man must not expect God to receive such because it is contrary to the nature of love.

The act of disobedience to God's command would not be an issue with Adam and Eve, and, in fact, could not have arisen had Adam and Eve not been endowed with a free will. Had God withheld this element of choice from man's make-up, He would have been rendered imperfect. Because He is perfect, He would not alter His Word. Man cannot be compelled to love against his will. God intended His command to them not to eat of the fruit of the Tree of Knowledge of Good and Evil as a test of their will. God clearly, specifically, and carefully made sure that both Adam and Eve understood the serious consequences of disobeying Him. There was no question about whether Eve had understood God's command, for she was able to repeat God's Word to Satan when he approached her as the serpent. Yet, in spite of this, Eve eventually chose to obey the serpent, a lesser being than herself, and a being that Adam had named. Likewise, Adam chose to obey his wife instead of God. Eve was deceived, but Adam was not. He chose to obey Eve rather than God.

CHAPTER 3

THE ENTRANCE
OF SIN

A n unexpected and unusual voice speaks to Eve's spirit. Adam was oblivious to it for it was a spirit-to-spirit communication. The voice is neither male nor female. It is penetrating and pernicious. The tone of the voice is above the octave of the highest natural note, and like an arrow filled with deadly poison, it travels to and through her being. Words spoken by the voice have a hypnotic, gripping, and compelling effect as they enter her being. She looks around to trace the source of this new voice that speaks within her. As she looks up, she sees, coiled around the branch of a tree above her head, a serpent from which the voice came. The serpent, though a beautiful and clever creature in itself, becomes the instrument of Satan, the master liar and deceiver, the originator of sin and evil.

Satan's intentions are multiple and cleverly set forth. He wants Eve to question God's intentions regarding her and Adam. His strategy is to distort the God-given Word and to cast doubt in Eve's mind in order to get her to disobey the Word of God. He wants her to think that he, Satan, is offering them more than what God has offered to them. He appeals to her humanness, manipulating her to indulge in self-love to get her to break

11

from the spirit of truth and God's love, and sever her union with God. Satan does so by offering her the elevated status of a god. He knows that if he gets her to act upon his word instead of God's, she would have submitted her allegiance to him instead of to God and, by doing so, Satan would have gained access into her mind and heart.

Satan wants their world—the earth—as well as their dominion and authority over it. He is powerless without their consent however, so he uses his power of deception to trick Eve into consenting. When Adam in turn consents, he forfeits his authority over the earth and Satan claims it by default. Satan knows the limitations of Eve's humanness as compared to the superiority of his spiritual existence. He knows so well that if he can get control of Eve's mind, he will also get control of her will. He knows her innocence and is well aware of his advantage over Eve, so he moves in without introduction or courtesy. He says to Eve:

> Yea, hath God said, Ye shall not eat of every tree of the garden?[2] And the woman said unto the serpent, We may eat of the fruit of the trees of the garden:[3] But of the fruit of the tree which is in the midst of the garden, God hath said, Ye shall not eat of it, neither shall ye touch it, lest ye die.[4] And the serpent said unto the woman, Ye shall not surely die:[5] For God doth know that in the day ye eat thereof, then your eyes shall be opened, and ye shall be as gods, knowing good and evil.
>
> —Genesis 3:1b-5

Eve succumbs to Satan's temptations and, as she encourages her husband Adam to eat of the fruit, he too gives in to his wife:

> [6] And when the woman saw that the tree was good for food, and that it was pleasant to the eyes, and a tree to be desired to make one wise, she took of the fruit thereof, and did eat, and gave also unto her husband with her; and he did eat.
>
> —Genesis 3:6

[Note: The understanding of what happened to Eve comes out of a personal experience that I had during the early years of my preparation for ministry. On this occasion, while I was volunteering at a telethon, Satan himself spoke to me. There is really no voice in this world with which to compare Satan's voice and this makes it difficult to describe.

As I picked up the phone, a high-pitched voice spoke to me from the other end of the telephone line. Its tone was higher than the highest note on the musical scale in the natural realm. Every word seemed to shoot through my being like a piercing arrow cutting into my flesh, and as if venomous poison charged with evil power was coursing through and through my body.

During the course of dialogue, I told Satan that he was a liar. This enraged him, and, as I kept repeating it, the angrier and more outraged he became. He protested, maintaining his rage, saying that Jesus Christ is the liar and that Jesus had stolen from him New York City, Los Angeles, London, other major cities and some nations of the world from him. I had the sense that he was ready to wage war against Jesus and his followers. As I continued, he became more and more furious and aggressively insisted that Jesus had done him wrong by stealing "his" dominion.

So as not to disturb the moderator on camera in the television studio, I had a momentary thought to end the conversation, and immediately, to my surprise, Satan said to me, "ah ha, you are afraid." In that instant, I received a word of knowledge from the Lord of Satan's swift discerning ability. This was a big surprise to me because I was not afraid. However, by it I understood that whenever a person has the smallest degree of doubt or unbelief or even the slightest hesitancy in his exercise of faith in Jesus

Christ or even a minuscule amount of fear of Satan, he discerns it and maintains a position of control and influence over that person.

Jesus Christ allowed me to have this experience knowing that it would serve a range of purposes in my life and ministry in bringing deliverance, healing and miracles to the lives of many, irrespective of distance.

This experience has given me a sense of what happened to Eve when Satan assailed her in the Garden of Eden and the debilitating and hypnotic effect that his voice had on her being. Man is defenseless under Satan's mastery of deception, lies, and evil power. Man's only defense against this diabolical creature is having Jesus Christ and the word of God well-established in his life.]

Disobedience to God is sin and so they had sinned against God. In this act of disobedience, they were unknowingly saying to God that He is not the supreme authority in their lives and that their loyalty and faith are not fully settled, rooted and grounded in God. Furthermore, though unintentionally, they demeaned, belittled, and dishonored God by treating Him with irreverence.

> **"** *God's Word does not always make sense because it does not always cater to the senses, but to the spirit.* **"**

When Adam and Eve disobeyed God's command not to eat of the Tree of Knowledge of Good and Evil, sin entered into man's life and into the world.

If Adam and Eve were only spirit beings like God or Satan, this line of deception would not have been so simple, but Satan appealed to Eve's natural senses. What Satan said to Eve seemed to make sense to her and she moved from God's word to her emotions and, in doing so, she moved from the spirit realm to the realm of senses where Satan was able to captivate her will.

To the human being, God's Word does not always make sense because it does not always cater to the senses, but to the spirit. God's word is spirit (John 6:63). Human senses are of the physical, flesh realm, and that realm limits man to the natural dimension. Man, being both spirit and flesh, has the choice to operate in both realms. If, when we hear the word of God, we process it in the natural sense realm, we disconnect from God and then lose the influence and power of the spirit realm. For example, when we read or hear the Word of God we unwittingly assess it in the natural realm where we process it through our senses, and this causes the Word of God to lose its effectiveness in us. We, therefore, can relate to the experiences of Adam and Eve because that is what happens to all of us on a daily basis. Thus, our hope for a spiritual result is unrealized. We say that God's Word is difficult to understand and that is because we transpose it from the spirit realm to the natural realm where we try to interpret it through our senses. Let us keep in mind that man lives in two realms simultaneously—the natural realm and the spirit realm. The spiritual realm, however, has the greater influence. Jesus used this teaching to illustrate the reality of the two realms.

> That which is born of the flesh is flesh; and that which is born of the Spirit is spirit.
>
> —John 3:6

We must not compromise the two natures. Each has its place and function to benefit us, and we need, therefore, to understand this God-given privilege and use each to our advantage, as God ordains it.

For they that are after the flesh do mind the things of the flesh; but they that are after the Spirit the things of the Spirit.[6] For to be carnally minded is death; but to be spiritually minded is life and peace.[7] Because the carnal mind is enmity against God: for it is not subject to the law of God, neither indeed can be.[8] So then they that are in the flesh cannot please God.

—Romans 8:5–8

Jesus, while on earth, was successful because He never compromised His two natures. Adam and Eve, however, certainly did. They did not understand that in order for a person to function successfully, he or she must not make spiritual things natural or natural things spiritual. God's Word is spirit and life and must remain so at all times. It loses its spiritual influence and power if it is made natural. Likewise, natural things are open to possible misinterpretation that may lead to deception when we interpret them in the spiritual realm. When we compromise our two natures, we leave ourselves open to the distortion of truth, which inevitably leads to failure. We must maintain the integrity of each of our two natures, appropriating spiritual things spiritually and natural things naturally. A good example of this is seen when Peter, a disciple of Jesus Christ, acted on Jesus' Word, without interpreting it in the sense realm, and thus walked on the Sea of Galilee, but the moment Peter engaged his senses he began to sink.

And in the fourth watch of the night Jesus went unto them, walking on the sea.[26] And when the disciples saw him walking on the sea, they were troubled, saying, It is a spirit; and they cried out for fear.[27] But straightway Jesus spake unto them, saying, Be of good cheer; it is I; be not afraid.[28] And Peter answered him and said, Lord, if it be thou, bid me come unto thee on the water.[29] And he said, Come. And when Peter was come down out of the ship, he walked on the water, to go to Jesus.[30] But when he saw the wind boisterous, he was afraid; and beginning to sink, he cried, saying, Lord, save me.[31] And immediately Jesus

stretched forth his hand, and caught him, and said unto him,
O thou of little faith, wherefore didst thou doubt?

—Matthew 14:25–31

Similarly, when Eve was operating in the spirit realm without compromise, she obeyed the Word of God and said to the serpent that she would not eat of the fruit of the tree. It was only when Eve moved from the spirit realm to the sense realm that Satan was able to influence her will, and thus she yielded her will to him. That which she heard, saw and reasoned (the sense realm) she directed her will to obey. In following her senses rather than obeying the Word of God, she compromised and did eat of the fruit of the tree.

The human being is such an advanced creation that only God, the Maker, fully understands the intricacies of its design. Humans have not been able to fully understand their own design. If we then place our reliance upon ourselves, we are bound to make mistakes, make wrong choices, and complicate the simplicity of obeying God, Who knows all things and wants the best for His children.

Many have judged Adam and Eve unjustly. By God's command not to eat of the Tree of the Knowledge of Good and Evil, they were aware that evil was a reality but they had no experiential knowledge of it. We have more knowledge and experience of good and evil than Adam and Eve had and we do the same as they did and worse, so to judge them is a case of the guilty judging the guilty. To the pure in heart, all things are pure. Because they were pure in heart, they expected everything and everyone to be pure in heart. Today, we have the knowledge of good and evil—of Satan, of his deceptive powers, and of his hatred toward us—and yet, we willingly and wholeheartedly obey him more than we obey God.

Nevertheless, God so loved mankind that He ordained a divine plan to bring man back into fellowship and sonship wherein man's birthright and dominion over the earth would be restored. Therein, the three Persons within God, the Trinity, would cooperate; each in a dispensation of time, each with an assigned purpose, until man returns to his original position, state, purpose, and dominion over the earth

SATAN SELF MADE

Let us take a moment to consider a subject that has long been controversial. Many have asked, "If God is sovereign, omniscient, and infallible, why would He allow Satan to do what he did to Adam and Eve? And why did He make Satan in the first place?" Please be informed, dear reader, that God did not create Satan, the devil.

God created an archangel named Lucifer, which meant *Son of the Morning*, because God had endowed Lucifer with such magnificent beauty. Lucifer held the elevated position of chief cherub, having charge over one third of heaven's angels, and was given the privilege to serve in the throne room of God. Lucifer's gifts included the making of music and the leading of heaven's angelic choir. This was Lucifer's rank, gift, and privilege. The other archangels are Michael and Gabriel, and they each had charge over one third of the angels. Heaven's order and structure saw God's plans and purposes carried out under the leadership of these three archangels.

Let us now visit heaven before the beginning of time to see this flawless archangel as God originally created him. Picture Lucifer conducting heaven's choirs in the very throne room of God, clothed in exquisite beauty, spectacularly adorned with the brilliance of every precious stone. Hear the sound of tabrets, pipes and other musical instruments exuding from his very being; its harmonious melody awe-inspiring in its purity. Lucifer was created to worship and he continuously offered superlative worship onto Omnipotence. He was perfect in the sight of God and all of heaven admired and respected him for his beauty, his brilliance, and his rank.

Lucifer, together with the other archangels Michael and Gabriel, served Almighty God honorably. They had the authority and responsibility of executing God's plans, each with one-third of the angels under their charge. How then is it possible for such a perfect creation to become corrupt? Let us now follow Lucifer as he gathers the angels under his command and descends to the earth, one of his assigned territories, to oversee its preparation for occupancy as God has instructed. Watch as he and his angels diligently carry out God's landscape design of earth. He is instrumental in the Garden of Eden knowing the placement of each tree, flowering plant and shrub that God created, including the Tree of Knowledge of Good and Evil and the Tree of Life. He knows the potential for anyone partaking of these trees.

Lucifer then hears the Trinity announce, "Let Us make man in Our image, after Our likeness" and turns to witness the Trinity tenderly and intricately fashioning "man"—a new creation—out of the dust of the earth, and naming him "Adam". Lucifer looks on in astonishment as God breathes His own breath into him and gives him life. This "Adam creature" comes alive, for he is now a living soul and, from the intense look of unadulterated love in Trinity's eyes, he is clearly the apple of His eye. The Trinity then declares, "Let *man* have dominion over the fish of the sea, and over the fowl of the air, and over the cattle, and over all the earth, and over every creeping thing that creepeth upon the earth." Lucifer could not believe that the Trinity was giving this dust creature dominion over all the earth. "I am the elder of God's creations," he thinks, and "I should be the rightful recipient of the dominion over planet earth, not this lesser being. After all, I possess far greater attributes as a spirit-being than this man made of dust." The more he dwells on what he has seen and heard, the more he covets Adam's position of dominion and the more consumed he becomes with pride, jealousy, envy and greed. As he opens his heart fully to these dark and ungodly feelings and emotions, his greed mushrooms and he lusts for even more power and dominion until it erupts into the most unholy desire . . . "I will be like the most High God."

Michael and Gabriel chose to remain loyal to their Creator and respected His creation, while Lucifer, with sin now in his heart, chose not to do so. For this act of treason, God stripped him of his beauty, rank, and power. The celebrated cherub, Lucifer, then became Satan, the devil, also called the old serpent and the dragon, and was relegated to live with the nature of sin, corruption, and evil, which he created in and of himself.

Sin, having been conceived in the super-angel, resulted in a corrupted nature that fostered even more greed and lust for more power. Hereafter,

Lucifer was no longer satisfied with being the chief cherub over the cherubim; no longer satisfied to be the anointed cherub and to lead heaven's celestial choir; no longer satisfied with having charge over one-third of the angels; no longer satisfied that he had the elevated privilege of serving in the throne room of God. The newly developed lust for dominion and rule eroded his love and loyalty towards God, which he replaced with pride, arrogance, and self-love. He became obsessed. Lust for dominion and power drove him and so he desired to rise above God and to sit upon His throne.

It does not seem possible that Lucifer could conceive sin while he was in heaven, although that is the universally accepted view.

God cannot be less than perfect; therefore, it is reasonable to presume that the environment in which He exists should also be perfect—holy and pure. How then can there be the possibility for sin or corruption in the Kingdom of Heaven? God's presence and perfection govern, permeate, and illuminate the entire heavenly realm, and everyone in heaven responds totally and completely to the purity and perfection that exist there. If Lucifer and the angels under his charge were in heaven when they sinned, we would have to wonder why no other angel before or after Lucifer and his angels sinned.

The following scriptures point us to a possible answer to this question and help us to understand the privilege that Lucifer had and subsequently lost.

> For thou hast said in thine heart, **I will ascend into heaven,** I will exalt my throne above the stars of God: I will sit also upon the mount of the congregation, in the sides of the north:[14] I will **ascend above the heights of the clouds;** I will be like the most High.
>
> —Isaiah 14:13–14 (bold print for emphasis)

Thou hast been in Eden the garden of God; every precious stone was thy covering, the sardius, topaz, and the diamond, the beryl, the onyx, and the jasper, the sapphire, the emerald, and the carbuncle, and gold: the workmanship of thy tabrets and of thy pipes was prepared in thee in the day that thou wast created.[14] Thou art the anointed cherub that covereth; and I have set thee so: **thou wast upon the holy mountain of God; thou hast walked up and down in the midst of the stones of fire.[15] Thou wast perfect in thy ways from the day that thou wast created, till iniquity was found in thee.[16]** By the multitude of thy merchandise they have filled the midst of thee with violence, and thou hast sinned: therefore **I will cast thee as profane out of the mountain of God:** and I will destroy thee, O covering cherub, **from the midst of the stones of fire.[17]** Thine heart was lifted up because of thy beauty, thou hast corrupted thy wisdom by reason of thy brightness: I will cast thee to the ground, I will lay thee before kings, that they may behold thee.[18] Thou hast defiled thy sanctuaries by the multitude of thine iniquities, by the iniquity of thy traffick; therefore will I bring forth a fire from the midst of thee, it shall devour thee, and **I will bring thee to ashes upon the earth in the sight of all them that behold thee.[19]** All they that know thee among the people shall be astonished at thee: thou shalt be a terror, and never shalt thou be any more.

—Ezekiel 28:13–19 (bold print for emphasis)

If Lucifer was in heaven, why would he say that he would ascend into heaven and above the heights of the clouds? To ascend you must be beneath. Scripture affirms that no one can enter into heaven with sin. (Galatians 5:19-21). The *holy mountain of God* cited in scripture refers to Mt. Sinai. The *stones of fire* refer to the refraction of sunlight from the precious stones that were on the surface of the earth at that time.

What a distortion of thought the brewing sin in Lucifer's heart had brought. His sin had made him stupid, just as sin makes every one of us. Sin erodes our intelligence, our reason, and our perception to such an extent, that it makes us think contrary to truth, and we believe a lie instead of the truth. Sin had erased from Lucifer's mind the knowledge of who God is, and that it was God who had made him the exalted archangel. This is ingratitude! Lucifer was beside himself, intoxicated with the sins of jealousy, greed, envy, pride, arrogance, hatred, and lust for power.

" God does not violate His own Word, nor does He infringe upon our free will. "

In his desire to overthrow God, Lucifer tried to enter heaven but God barred him and expelled him, together with the one-third of the angels that had joined Lucifer in his rebellion against God. Since Lucifer committed the sins of pride, jealousy, greed, and rebellion on earth, God's law necessitated Lucifer's extradition to earth in the process of his sentencing. Whatever action Adam would have taken against Lucifer/Satan, God would have endorsed. Instead, Eve gave in to Satan's deception and Adam, by choice, yielded his headship to his wife. God would not permit Satan's entrance into heaven. Heaven is a holy place and God must act. It was for Satan's ultimate judgment, along with his followers, that God created hell.

Was this a cruel act on God's part, knowing that His children were on earth and Satan's sinful nature might affect them? No, it was not. While that possibility does exist, God will neither shield us nor prevent us from exercising our duty and responsibility to live by His Word as He has commanded us to do. God never infringes upon the exercise of our free will. When we choose to live by His Word, God's eternal law provides for our total protection and well-being.

" God's Word is His will. "

Did God know that Adam would have disobeyed Him, and thus fall into sin? Yes, He certainly did, but God's foreknowledge does not make Him alter His state of perfection. God only intervenes proactively in man's affairs when His beloved sons, who are given dominion over the earth and are carrying out His purposes, make request of Him through prayer, supplication, or intercession that are in line with His divine will and plan. We are obliged to operate within His will, as He makes it known. God could not interfere with Adam's choice or alter his decision. God does not violate His own Word, nor does He infringe upon our free will. Furthermore, the host of angels and all of God's creations perpetually witness God's integrity in His dealings and responses in every situation. God upholds His laws by His unchanging Word, character, and nature. God's Word is His will. God's Word is not subject to alteration or change. He is infallible, holy, and perfect. Indeed, God's thoughts are higher than our thoughts and His ways are higher than our ways. If it were not so, He would not be God.

> For as the heavens are higher than the earth, so are my ways higher than your ways, and my thoughts than your thoughts.
> —Isaiah 55:9

Should there be any questioning or accusation against God on your part, let it be in the fact that He retains His perfection, His holiness and His righteousness, and, as such, accepts the choice of man and angels to voluntarily love and obey Him or not, and to love and obey whomever they choose. God is love, and love is the freewill expression to honor, reverence, and obey whosoever we will.

The very act of questioning God is in itself irreverent, disrespectful, and dishonorable to God and serves to confirm that man has indeed inherited Satan's corrupt nature. One does not have the right to question his Maker—the One who gave him his life, his breath, his faculties, and his speech. Man must know that God is not obliged to give any further proof of Himself and of His actions to those who He has created.

Nay but, O man, who art thou that repliest against God? Shall the thing formed say to him that formed it, Why hast thou made me thus?[21] Hath not the potter power over the clay, of the same lump to make one vessel unto honour, and another unto dishonour?

—Romans 9:20–21

Those who live in defiance of God's Word and who set out to oppose God and to attempt to disqualify Him from being holy and just, have successfully illuminated Satan's fingerprint upon their hearts and minds. The attempt to judge and disqualify God is the mark of fallen man. The fact is that our very existence certifies that God exists and is supreme over life, the world, and everything in it. Creation itself declares His marvelous handiwork.

In keeping with the generic law of God that everything produces after its own kind, Adam's sin nature that he received from Satan was passed on to us, his offspring. We all are born with this sinful nature, and that is why a parent does not have to teach a child to misbehave or be rebellious. That tendency is at the essence of his or her nature. God is ever so aware of this disadvantage that, in spite of man's unfounded questioning of Him, God has gone about answering man's questions.

DEATH BEGINS TO REIGN

The moment Eve and Adam disobeyed God and ate from the Tree of Knowledge of Good and Evil, death began to reign in them. Spiritual death was instant when their spirits separated from God, the source of their spiritual being. Physical death is a slow process, as the body no longer functions in total harmony with its environment. From that time on, the body started to degenerate and to eventually lose its ability to function and exist. It would eventually return to the earth from whence it came.

24

What a reality shock it must have been for Adam and Eve when instantly there was no more connection to God. With no Spirit-to-spirit connection with God, they now had to rely upon their natural senses as the order of their being changed from spirit-soul-body to that of body-soul-spirit. In this reversed order, Adam and Eve found it impossible to communicate with God, for their senses, from that moment on, had become their dominant personality. For the first time, Adam and Eve saw themselves as naked, ashamed, and afraid. Adam then took leaves from a fig tree and made "aprons"—loin coverings for himself and for his wife (Genesis 3:7). God never wanted them to experience evil, and this is why He commanded them not to eat from the Tree of Knowledge of Good and Evil. He never intended that His children would separate from Him. He had made them for His pleasure and to share His nature, character and his blessings. Now the sin of disobedience had separated them from Him.

> *" God is never taken by surprise. He knows all things at the same time, and even before the heart conceives them. "*

Adam had unwittingly relinquished his dominion and authority over the earth to Satan, in this act of disobedience to God, by taking sides with Satan against God's command. Adam and Eve were to live in misery, shame, and defeat; robbed of the dignity, power, and authority that were their birthright. Satan had finally accomplished his goal to claim dominion and act as god over the earth. He outmatched Adam and Eve with his deceptive abilities. His victory, though, was hollow since God relegated Satan to rule from darkness. Satan, even today, wields the rod of fear and intimidation from the shadows of the earth rather than in the open. Satan is hated and despised rather than adored, revered, and glorified as we adore, revere, and glorify God, the true King and Ruler of the earth. Satan, once the "Son of the Morning" became the *Prince of Darkness*. Although Satan had the right to rule on the earth, God reduced him to operate like a phantom on the earth rather than as a king. He became a hideous creature of darkness condemned to live in the shadows, lurking behind the scenes, always hiding behind a mask of fallen man, unable to show his true self because of the ugliness of his being.

On God's next visit to the garden, Adam and Eve were not at their regular meeting place to greet Him. They were hiding from God.

> And the LORD God called unto Adam, and said unto him, Where art thou?
>
> —Genesis 3:9

Understand that when God asks a question, it is not that He does not know the answer. He simply gives the individual an opportunity to express himself and participate.

> And he (Adam) said, I heard thy voice in the garden, and I was afraid, because I was naked; and I hid myself.[11] And he said, Who told thee that thou wast naked? Hast thou eaten of the tree, whereof I commanded thee that thou shouldest not eat?[12] And the man said, The woman whom thou gavest to be with me, she gave me of the tree, and I did eat.[13] And the LORD God said unto the woman, What is this that thou hast done? And the woman said, The serpent beguiled me, and I did eat.
>
> —Genesis 3:10–13

Was God surprised? No, God cannot be surprised. He is omniscient. He knows everything at the same time, even before it happens. However, because of His perfect nature, God allows natural things to take their natural course, and spiritual things to take their spiritual course. God alone can do this because He has the ability to turn every defeat into greater victory for our benefit and for His, and, in doing so, He lets all creation see His goodness, His fairness, His kindness, His mercy, His love, His infallibility, His omniscience, and His omnipotence. This will result in creation's continued voluntary love for the perfect and eternal God that He is. He created time and space, the land and sea, vegetation and matter, man and animal, the visible and the invisible, kingdoms, planets and galaxies. He is always in control. God is never taken by surprise. He knows all things at the same time, and even before the heart conceives them.

> ¹⁴ And the LORD God said unto the serpent, Because thou hast done this, thou art cursed above all cattle, and above every beast of the field; upon thy belly shalt thou go, and dust shalt thou eat all the days of thy life:¹⁵ And I will put enmity between thee and the woman, and between thy seed and her seed; it shall bruise thy head, and thou shalt bruise his heel.
> —Genesis 3:14-15

Adam and Eve had to face the consequences of their sin:

> ¹⁶ Unto the woman he said, I will greatly multiply thy sorrow and thy conception; in sorrow thou shalt bring forth children; and thy desire shall be to thy husband, and he shall rule over thee.¹⁷ And unto Adam he said, Because thou hast hearkened unto the voice of thy wife, and hast eaten of the tree, of which I commanded thee, saying, Thou shalt not eat of it: cursed is the ground for thy sake; in sorrow shalt thou eat of it all the days of thy life;¹⁸ Thorns also and thistles shall it bring forth to thee; and thou shalt eat the herb of the field;¹⁹ In the sweat of thy face shalt thou eat bread, till thou return unto the ground; for out of it wast thou taken: for dust thou art, and unto dust shalt thou return.²⁰ And Adam called his wife's name Eve; because she was the mother of all living.²¹ Unto Adam also and to his wife did the LORD God make coats of skins, and clothed them.
> —Genesis 3:16–21

Adam and Eve's attempt to cover their sin was futile. Sinful man cannot save himself from sin. Sin is in the heart and nature. Sinfulness cannot make atonement for sin. Only sinlessness can atone for sin and so, in their sinful state, their own attempt to cover themselves with fig leaves could not succeed.

God would now begin to activate His redemptive plan towards man's restoration and wholeness.

In God's law, there is no remission of sin without the shedding of blood. Therefore, God shed the blood of an animal to make atonement for Adam and Eve's sin, and, with the skin of the animal, He covered their nakedness as a reminder to them that God takes life and sheds blood to make atonement for sin. Yet, the blood of animals simply covered their sin but could not remove it. This too was a temporary measure. God would one day provide a perfect, sinless, human substitute, who would willingly shed His sinless blood for the remission of man's sin.

God Himself would condescend through His Word, the Second Person in the Trinity, to take on the form of man after the order of Adam, and would give His life as the penalty for man's sin in order to redeem man and bring him back into relationship and fellowship with the Father.

God loved Adam and Eve in spite of their failure. He loves His children and always will, but He hates the sin in them which separates them from Him and leaves them subject to Satan and in a state of defeat. Love would not leave them in that state. In time, God's love would redeem them and would restore them to their original state and purpose.

THE LESSON

❝ Life without God is emptiness and leaves a void that nothing and no one but He can fill. ❞

Adam and Eve were banished from the Garden of Eden as a result of their sin. They must now live without the Presence of God, as their spirit is now separate from God. They must plant their own garden and grow their own crops for food to feed themselves and their offspring. They must experience the consequences of sin so they can teach their children the importance of obeying God and that man should not live by bread alone, but by every word that proceeds from the mouth of God—bread being food for the natural man and God's word being food for the spirit man. They would teach their offspring that whatsoever they sow, they also must reap; that if they would reject God, God would have to accept their choice and that life without God is emptiness and leaves a void that nothing and no one but He can fill. Adam and Eve would further explain to their offspring that Satan is now the self-appointed god of the earth, having stolen their birthright, their earth, and their dominion. Further, they would explain that Satan is a fallen angel, banned from entering heaven because he rebelled against God and lost his exalted position. They would explain that Satan is loveless, without compassion and mercy, evil and cruel and that he hates God and man. In addition, they would learn that although Satan cannot directly hurt God, he can indirectly do so by hurting man, who is the apple of God's eye. From God's prophetic word, Adam and Eve would teach their children that God would one day rescue them from Satan's rule over their lives as He promised.

> And I will put enmity between thee and the woman, and between thy seed and her seed; it shall bruise thy head, and thou shalt bruise his heel.
>
> —Genesis 3:15

The heel of the seed of the woman, one of Adam and Eve's offspring, would bruise the serpent's head as a mark of Satan's defeat. Adam and Eve would tell their children that God's prophetic word is now the only hope for mankind, and that they are determined to live by the Word of God.

They would urge their children to do the same in order to please God and have His favor and blessing. One can imagine Adam and Eve's deep remorse at the choice they made that separated them from their God and the anguish they must feel at the emptiness of their new existence bound by their senses. It may seem that whatever God had planned through Adam for mankind was set back, but God would eventually accomplish His purpose. God cannot lose or fail.

CHAPTER 4

GOD'S JUSTICE

God is Perfection. His justice operates out of His word given for man to live by. Justice is a part of God's very nature. It is that characteristic of God that made Him place within the life of angel and man a free will, even though He foreknew that they could and would use it against themselves, and against Him. For God to withhold or restrict their freedom of choice would be contrary to His perfect nature.

The subject of God's justice seems to be beyond our understanding and is determined by God's sovereignty—a mystery of its own. I must therefore make careful note that we are here examining the concept of God's justice within the restricted context of this book.

Omnipotence and Omniscience execute perfect justice at all times and in all circumstances, without any limitations or boundaries, without any violation of His love and perfection. God is not intimidated by any situation that may arise, nor is He incapable of resolving any issue that His own creation might bring upon themselves, whether good or evil. Neither would His perfection be influenced by His foreknowledge of the action of angels and men. He is the Supreme Being!

Justice is inherent in every single law of God. It is also a component of the free-will concept and responds appropriately to the law of good and evil, right and wrong, holy and unholy, innocence and guilt; so that whatever choice angel or man may make, justice responds perfectly. If they sow that which is evil, they reap evil: corruption, jealousy, hate, sickness, distress, failure, unhappiness, and separation from the presence of God. If they sow that which is good, they reap good: health, peace, victory, success, blessing, happiness, and the continuance of God's favor.

For example, the law of justice is inherent in God's Ten Commandments, for the appropriate law of justice is applied, executing cursing on the disobedient and blessings on the obedient. God does not have to sit on His judgment seat and judge individual cases and nations. This is automatically executed by His law of justice, based on His eternal unchangeable Word and determined as we exercise our free choice. Angels and man, therefore, decide their own fate based on God's given word.

> I call heaven and earth to record this day against you, that I have set before you life and death, blessing and cursing: therefore choose life that both thou and thy seed may live:
> —Deuteronomy 30:19

> And afterward he read all the words of the law, the blessings and cursings, according to all that is written in the book of the law.
> —Joshua 8:34

> And this is the condemnation, that light is come into the world, and men loved darkness rather than light, because their deeds were evil."
> —John 3:19

Justice that is within God's Law weighs the facts, circumstances and motives surrounding the offence and it rules accordingly. It also takes into account God's plans and purposes. Let us consider the rulings in the case of two of God's creations—the archangel, Lucifer and the first man and woman, Adam and Eve. Lucifer was one of the three archangels given the privilege of serving in the throne room of God. Similarly, Adam and

Eve were God's greatest earthly creation and work of art, in whom God placed His own image and likeness, and gave them planet earth as their own. Both Lucifer and God's first children were privileged, special, created beings of God.

I find two aspects of God's justice applied in the case of Lucifer and Adam and Eve. In the case of Lucifer, there was no reprieve considered on his sentence for treason and murder. This was so because Lucifer soberly, consciously, and deliberately used his free will to corrupt himself allowing iniquity to enter his heart. With this condition of heart, he tried to exalt himself above God, thereby violating God's universal law and order which set God as Supreme and which govern all of creation. In so doing, he corrupted himself and went on to corrupt Adam and Eve, bringing sin and death to mankind. Lucifer was not deceived. Nor was he innocent. He had forfeited the honor God had bestowed upon him and the privilege of sharing the divine life. This was his choice and justice must follow, and it did. He brought upon himself the sentence of eternal punishment which will take place in the Lake of Fire prepared for him and the angels that supported him.

**" Sin metes out its own judgment
without God's inclusion. "**

In the case of Adam and Eve, however, they were granted a reprieve because of their innocence. Adam and Eve were deceived and violated by Lucifer, now called Satan, whose intent was to inflict evil, corruption, and death upon them. Satan's act was directed at God more than it was directed toward Adam and Eve. Satan wanted them to sin against God and to mar the image and likeness of God in them so that he could then have a claim on the earth by default. He took advantage of their innocence, their inexperience, their purity of heart, and he deceived them. Because Adam and Eve did not have full knowledge and understanding of what they were coerced into doing, they did not soberly, deliberately, and consciously direct their free will to challenge God's universal law and corrupt His established order. Note, however, that their innocence did not exempt them from the consequences of disobeying God's specific instructions to them. Justice that is within God's Law weighs the facts, circumstances and motives surrounding the offence and it rules. The verdict imposed the penalty of expulsion from the Garden of Eden. This also meant a life without relationship, fellowship, and dialogue with God, as well as strenuous labor for the rest of their life until their flesh, which is now corrupted, would degenerate, die, and go back to the earth. If the imposed penalty is paid with sinless blood, their spirit can again be reunited with God. If not, it will be eternally separated from God and go into Satan's Lake of Fire.

All of creation looked on with keen interest at the method of justice that God would apply. God's justice is not carried out in terms of human knowledge and response, based on right and wrong, good and bad, partiality and impartiality, favor or disfavor. God bases it on the principle of individual choice and consequence. The offence, therefore, determines the course of justice and, as such, God can never be accused of injustice. Justice, being an element of the free will, exempts God from any charge of partiality or injustice. This is why when Lucifer and Adam and Eve chose to violate God's law, in spite of their position and privilege, God could not withhold justice from taking its course.

Sin metes out its own judgment without God's inclusion. This is an inherent principle in God's law of cause and effect. When we obey God's law, which is His Word, the inherency of blessings—goodwill, peace, prosperity, and happiness—follow. When we disobey His law, the inherency of cursing is applied and sorrow, pain, distress, sickness, and failure follow. Most of the time, God is silent and allows consequential justice to run its course. However, there is a time when God verbalizes a prescribed judgment for the benefit of creation and for establishing a record of the consequences of sin for our learning and example.

God's righteousness demanded that there be a penalty for sin. As man is an extension of God by virtue of His image and likeness seeded in him,

God could rightfully and justifiably pay the penalty for man's sin; and in His love, He did.

> For God so loved the world that he gave his only begotten Son, that whosoever believeth in him should not perish, but have everlasting life.
>
> —John 3:16

God is creation's example of perfection, holiness and justice and cannot be otherwise. All of creation would crumble if His justice was determined by His emotions or anything that would result in inconsistencies. God's justice, however, is established through His eternal, unchangeable Word.

CHAPTER 5

REALIZING ONE'S TRUE STATE

*" God is not what man thinks that
He is and makes Him to be. "*

Man can only accommodate God in his spirit when it is free from sin and alive to God. With the loss of that Spirit-to-spirit dimension, man now operates purely out of his physical senses, thus making fellowship and dialogue with God difficult.

God, above all, knows of the existing boundaries of man's senses. Man, however, had to accept the fact that he is simply not able to communicate with God while operating from the flesh (his senses). Man's natural eyes cannot see God because He is a Spirit; neither do they have the capacity to contain Him because of the brilliance of His glory. God must awaken man's awareness to the limitations of his fleshly existence and bring him to a place where he accepts this fact. Only then might he accept his limitations, and desire to submit to God's plan of redemption.

> **" *Man cannot make or create anything greater than himself.* "**

Dispossessed of that Spirit-to-spirit connection with God, man gropes around in blind disorder and confusion like a fish flounders outside of its natural habitat in an insanely desperate struggle to survive. In this state, man gullibly embraces anything and anyone offering a glimmer of hope for reconciliation with God, no matter how misleading and deceptive. Such schemes, ideologies, and philosophies never lead to God and cannot, because God is not what man thinks that He is and makes Him to be. At the failure and disappointment of each successive attempt to fill the void within himself, man seeks for another solution and then yet another, and would even create his own god or gods. He convinces himself that these gods, made with his imperfect, sinful hands, are divine, holy, and sacred and are able to meet his spiritual, moral, and social needs. Disconnected from God, man's intelligence and reason shrink to such a point that he is unable to see that a man cannot make or create anything greater than himself.

Oh, how terrible sin is and how cunningly masterful is sin's instigator, the devil!

***

Before God made Adam and Eve, He foresaw their fall and had ordained a plan of redemption that would involve the extension of Himself through His Word and His Spirit. Together, the Trinity would co-operate to bring about man's redemption and, in so doing, God would restore the relationship between Himself and man that was severed through Adam's sin. As we follow the role of each Person of the Trinity, we would clearly see the wisdom of God and the necessity of each Person of the Trinity in bringing about man's redemption.

Although scripture documents the role of the Trinity in the plan of redemption, God kept the orchestration of this plan veiled from our understanding until the present time. Why does He choose to reveal it at this time?

This is a time when man's values are guided by the philosophy, "If it feels good, do it." Modern ideologies, such as secular humanism and political correctness, have replaced what is right in the sight of God. Extreme rebellion is everywhere and abject immorality and heinous, unheard-of crime seem to be the order of the day. The family unit has long become defunct with the children in control of the parents, having received the sanction of the authorities for their dishonorable behavior. God is nowhere to be found. Men have become gods in themselves with the advent of the New Age movement. This is the maturing of times and, in keeping with God's schedule, it is a perfect time for God to reveal another mystery; for another world revival to break forth; and for bringing forth the greatest harvest of souls into the Kingdom of God before the return of Jesus Christ to earth.

***

CHAPTER 6

THE FIRST DISPENSATION: GOD THE FATHER

THE UNFOLDING OF THE MYSTERY BEGINS . . .

The First Person of the Trinity, God the Father, now initiates the first stage of the Trinity's plan of redemption for mankind. God's objective is to steer man away from relying upon his senses and to secure man's trust in Him as the *Invisible God.*

A COVENANT OF SUPERNATURAL FAITH ESTABLISHED

To accomplish this objective, God's wisdom necessitates that He must first choose a man with whom he could establish a *covenant of faith,* that is, a man who, in spite of his inability to see God with the natural eye, would believe God and accept the reality of His existence.

Abram was that chosen one, a seventy-five-year-old man who lived in Haran, a town in Mesopotamia, Iraq. Abram, a heathen and idol worshipper, responded to that call and God, therefore, directed him through the realm of supernatural faith.

> Now the LORD had said unto Abram, Get thee out of thy country, and from thy kindred, and from thy father's house, unto a land that I will shew thee:[2] And I will make of thee a great nation, and I will bless thee, and make thy name great; and thou shalt be a blessing:[3] And I will bless them that bless thee, and curse him that curseth thee: and in thee shall all families of the earth be blessed.[4] So Abram departed, as the LORD had spoken unto him;
>
> —Genesis 12:1–4

As Abram continued to rely on and obey God he grew in faith and relationship with his *Invisible God.* At age ninety-nine, God established a covenant of faith with him changing his name from Abram to Abraham (Father of Many Nations), God Himself pledging to bless him and his descendants if they walked in obedience to Him. God said:

> I am the Almighty God; walk before me, and be thou perfect. [2] And I will make my covenant between me and thee, and will multiply thee exceedingly. [3] And Abram fell on his face: and God talked with him, saying, [4] As for me, behold, my covenant is with thee, and thou shalt be a father of many nations. [5] Neither shall thy name any more be called Abram, but thy name shall be Abraham; for a father of many nations have I made thee. [6] And I will make thee exceeding fruitful, and I will make nations of thee, and kings shall come out of thee. [7] And I will establish my covenant between me and thee and thy seed after thee in their generations for an everlasting covenant, to be a God unto thee, and to thy seed after

thee. ⁸ And I will give unto thee, and to thy seed after thee, the land wherein thou art a stranger, all the land of Canaan, for an everlasting possession; and I will be their God. ⁹ And God said unto Abraham, Thou shalt keep my covenant therefore, thou, and thy seed after thee in their generations.

—Genesis 17:1-9

God's intention was to raise up a great nation through Abraham that would operate by faith and through which the Trinity would work to re-establish relationship with man. That great nation is Israel, and to Abraham and his descendants, God continued to make Himself known as the *Invisible God*. Through the Israelites the rest of the world will eventually know Him as God, Creator of Heaven and Earth—Man's Maker.

Through God's engineering, Abraham and his descendants lived in Egypt which, at that time, was the most powerful nation on the earth. Forced into slave labor, they worked long, hard hours in the most inhumane of conditions. God's plan was carried out through this diabolical plot of Satan whose intention was to break their will. Yet, in spite of their burdens, the Jews continued to look heavenward, holding fast to Jehovah, their *Invisible God*, believing and trusting in Him. Generation after generation they beseeched God for deliverance from their cruel bondage, but He remained silent. From a natural perspective, it would seem that God did not care for them enough to come to their rescue the moment they besought Him. It was not that God was uncaring or unable to deliver them; He was training them to live not just by "bread alone", that is, not to rely only on their natural senses, but live by faith in His Covenant with them. For four hundred and thirty years this continued until God was finally satisfied that He had indeed prepared a people of faith, worthy to be called His people.

Affliction and tribulation in slavery tried and tested the faith of the Jews and God found them to be loyal and faithful to Him, although they neither saw nor heard Him. They had come to believe in and accept Jehovah, the *Invisible God,* not through their senses, but through divine knowledge of His Person, which He revealed to them by His Spirit because of the covenant of faith established with them through Abraham.

God was satisfied that through this people He could orchestrate a divine plan to redeem mankind and restore man's relationship with Him. Within this plan God would fulfill His prophetic declaration of raising up the "seed of the woman" that would one day "bruise the serpent's head." Thus, God was ready to deliver His people from bondage in Egypt and release them into His divine master plan of restoration, reconciliation and redemption for all of mankind.

A Deliverer is Born

" Unique men must combine a unique fate with unique experiences to step into their unique destinies. "

God's next move was unprecedented, a move that only the *Divine Mind* could formulate. God began to manifest His power and glory to His people in a manner that astounded the natural mind as they began to grasp the almightiness of their God.

He could not manifest to them His Person because in their natural state they would not be able to contain Him. In His infinite wisdom, He had come up with the perfect plan. For this, God ordained the birth of a unique individual and endowed him with the heart and passion to be a deliverer. This special, divine endowment was seeded in his spirit to the degree that he would willingly give his life to fulfill the destiny embedded within him. His heart burned with passion to know God, to discover his destiny and to fulfill it. His earthly parents had no claim on his life, nor were they able to form any attachment to him. He was solely God's chosen vessel, chosen to be God's channel through whom He would save the Jews from their slavery in Egypt. He was not the *Seed of promise* that would bruise the serpent's head but he was the chosen deliverer of the people through whom that *Seed* would come.

Meanwhile, Satan, observing God's move, was gripped by panic and fear to the point of desperation. He was full of apprehension that this *seed* of the woman would bruise his head. He dreaded the thought of losing his short-lived rule on the earth. He feared for his ultimate fate and existence. Satan, having taken counsel with his demons, and realizing that they did not know who the child was, set out on a maniacal mission to eradicate this threat by any means possible, using the hand of Pharaoh himself to implement his diabolical plan.

Influenced by these demon spirits, Pharaoh's soothsayers notified him that this deliverer was born. Pharaoh sent his henchmen armed with swords on a rampage through the Jewish settlement, murdering every newborn, male child in the hope of ending the life of the deliverer. In the heat of the massacre, God kept this *child-deliverer* through his mother who hid him for three months and who, when she could hide him no more, placed him in a basket and set it afloat on the river Nile. With only love in her heart for her child, she somehow knew that to save him she must let him go, placing his fate entirely in the hands of God. What would cause a mother to take such unusual action? Omnipotence was working on her heart and she had to respond. By God's divine intervention, Pharaoh's daughter Bythia, who was childless and had yearned for a child, was bathing in the river Nile on the very path of this baby's *boat of destiny.* She drew the baby out of the river Nile and adopted him as her own. Bythia must have been praying to the Nile god to bless her with a child to fill the void in her life. The Nile god could not fulfill her wish but God, in His divine wisdom and omnipotence, accommodated her request and sent her, by way of the Nile, His child deliverer to nurture, care for, and love. She called the child Moses because one meaning of that name is "to draw out," since she had Moses drawn out of the river, but she was unaware of the true meaning of his name—*Deliverer!*

Through divine providence, the one who would one day defy and defeat Pharaoh and free his slaves was raised in his very palace, loved by him as his favored grandson, educated in all the ways, wisdom and knowledge of the Egyptians, and trained to rule in preference over Pharaoh's own son. This most feared enemy of Egypt had become the most loved prince of Egypt and heir to the throne.

> And Pharaoh charged all his people, saying, Every son that is born ye shall cast into the river, and every daughter ye shall save alive.
>
> —Exodus 1:22

And there went a man of the house of Levi, and took to wife a daughter of Levi.[2] And the woman conceived, and bare a son: and when she saw him that he was a goodly child, she hid him three months.[3] And when she could no longer hide him, she took for him an ark of bulrushes, and daubed it with slime and with pitch, and put the child therein; and she laid it in the flags by the river's brink.[4] And his sister stood afar off, to wit what would be done to him.[5] And the daughter of Pharaoh came down to wash herself at the river; and her maidens walked along by the river's side; and when she saw the ark among the flags, she sent her maid to fetch it.[6] And when she had opened it, she saw the child: and, behold, the babe wept. And she had compassion on him, and said, This is one of the Hebrews' children.[7] Then said his sister to Pharaoh's daughter, Shall I go and call to thee a nurse of the Hebrew women, that she may nurse the child for thee?[8] And Pharaoh's daughter said to her, Go. And the maid went and called the child's mother.[9] And Pharaoh's daughter said unto her, Take this child away, and nurse it for me, and I will give thee thy wages. And the woman took the child, and nursed it.[10] And the child grew, and she brought him unto Pharaoh's daughter, and he became her son. And she called his name Moses: and she said, Because I drew him out of the water.

—Exodus 2:1–10

God, in exercising His omnipotence and supremacy, preserved His "child deliverer" in the midst of the bloodshed. Divine providence was once again at work. Unique men must combine a unique fate with unique experiences to step into their unique destinies.

God's infallibility, omniscience and omnipotence are awesome and clearly revealed in this extraordinary account, although this is only a small display of His ability. God obviously and convincingly outwitted Satan. In his crazed, enraged state Satan was clueless of the fact that all the while, the very one he had raised up to destroy God's deliverer was the one responsible for his growth, development and well-being. The Trinity's plan for the restoration of man was in progress.

GOD CALLS MOSES

As Moses grew, he did not understand his compassion for the Jews and his longing to see them free from the bondage of slavery. He did not understand the deep-rooted impulse that propelled him in his passion for justice for the Jews. He did not know who he was or what his purpose was. His identity remained veiled to him as, step by step, God continued to mold in him, the required characteristics that would shape his life in order for him to fulfill his destiny. As the prince of Egypt, educated in Pharaoh's courts, Moses learned all the ways of the Egyptians. Little did he know that this was part of the training for his divine purpose.

Omnipotence was putting together His perfect will in His perfect way to fashion a deliverer through whom the *Seed* would come.

One day, driven by his great compassion for the slaves, Moses, upon witnessing an Egyptian taskmaster abusing a Jewish slave, impulsively rose up and killed the Egyptian, in defense of the slave. Moses had to flee Egypt because Pharaoh, who had once loved him as his beloved grandson, now wanted to kill him because of his one act against an Egyptian of lower rank. Omnipotence continued to work His plan in this sudden decision by Pharaoh to turn on the one in whom he had invested so much time grooming to be the next prince of Egypt. God had given him favor and acceptance with the Midianites and he lived with the family of Jethro, a priest and leader among them, who believed in the *Invisible God,* whom they referred to as the "God with no name." God kept Moses forty years in the wilderness of Midian to continue His work in Moses to step into his destiny despite Satan's every attempt to abort God's plan.

As Moses was tending Jethro's sheep one day, he saw an intensely brilliant glow at the summit of Mount Horeb and felt drawn to investigate. On reaching the summit, he encountered a bush on fire, yet the fire did not consume it. Out of the flames, the voice of God spoke into his spirit.

The occurrence of God speaking into the spirit of man had ceased with the separation of God and Adam and Eve in the Garden. However, on rare occasions, God, by His divine call and appointment of a few specially chosen individuals, would make an exception for the purpose of keeping the knowledge of Himself alive. He may also do so in the execution of His plan to restore man's relationship with Him. He did this with men like Job, Enoch, Abraham, Isaac, Jacob, Noah, and others—and now Moses.

God immediately introduced Himself to Moses as the God of his forefathers, Abraham, Isaac, and Jacob—the *Invisible God* to whom the Israelites had been praying for deliverance and in whom they had put their faith.

> And the LORD said, I have surely seen the affliction of my people which are in Egypt, and have heard their cry by reason of their taskmasters; for I know their sorrows;[8] And I am come down to deliver them out of the hand of the Egyptians, and to bring them up out of that land unto a good land and a large, unto a land flowing with milk and honey; unto the place of the Canaanites, and the Hittites, and the Amorites, and the Perizzites, and the

Hivites, and the Jebusites.[9] Now therefore, behold, the cry of the children of Israel is come unto me: and I have also seen the oppression wherewith the Egyptians oppress them.[10] Come now therefore, and I will send thee unto Pharaoh, that thou mayest bring forth my people the children of Israel out of Egypt.

—Exodus 3:7–10

Reluctant at first to face Pharaoh, but encouraged by God's mentoring and command, Moses left Midian. Armed only with his shepherd's rod and the knowledge that the true and living God who had commissioned him was with him, he headed out to confront Pharaoh in Egypt with the message from Jehovah to "let my people go."

Pharaoh bluntly refused and instead went on to impose greater burdens upon the slaves as an act of defiance to Moses and his newfound God.

Little did Pharaoh realize that God knew his heart and would work through the condition of his heart to draw him and Satan, the one who controlled him, into a showdown whereby all of Egypt would witness the power and might of Jehovah. Furthermore, at their defeat, Jehovah's name and the testimony of His power would spread throughout the world to the benefit of all the generations to come.

Through Moses, Jehovah continued to challenge Satan and his empire in Egypt, making an open show of him, humiliating him and exposing the fallacy of other gods. Satan was utterly outmatched and publicly defeated through repeated displays of Jehovah's unparalleled, supernatural power, as plague after plague followed Pharaoh's stubborn refusal to let God's people go. Jehovah triumphantly and spectacularly brought His people out of Satan's bondage and overthrew the most powerful nation in the world using just one man and a shepherd's rod.

Pharaoh, forced to finally acknowledge the validity and power of Moses' God, called for Moses by night and urged him to take his people and hasten out of Egypt. The Egyptian people themselves, anxious for them to leave, hurriedly brought them much gold and fine linen. So it was that the Israelites' faith in Jehovah, their *Invisible God,* had secured their release from 430 years of cruel bondage.

The mighty nation of Egypt was finally in shambles: the economy completely ruined by the death of most of the livestock and fish; the multiple gods all toppled and destroyed; the land reeking of the stench of death and decay. As dawn approached, the once proud and haughty Egyptians, now meek and trembling with the fearful impact of Jehovah fresh on their minds, simply stood by, powerless, as over two million slaves queued up to leave Egypt, taking with them what God wanted them to have to start that new way of life. The Jews, now freed from the bonds of slavery, gathered in abundance the gold, silver, fine linen, livestock, and nursery plants that once belonged to their former slave masters, and, with songs of joy and jubilation, marched out of Egypt with no one to stop them.

What a glorious day it was: the culmination of 430 years of relentless toiling, brutal beatings, weeping and supplication to God, now transformed into a jubilant victory march out of Egypt! The Israelites, a people without a country, denied of a land they could call their own and with no source of livelihood, set out on their journey to the Promised Land knowing that Jehovah their God was with them. Soon they would present themselves to Jehovah and they would see Him face to face, they thought. All they had was each other and their absolute faith in Jehovah to sustain them and to direct their lives as He sees fit. They were now totally dependent on Jehovah and this was His plan for their lives.

God's divine engineering to have a people who would believe ultimately in Him, not through the exercise of their natural senses but wholly through the spiritual dimension of faith, had yielded the response that He set out to accomplish. The wheels were in motion for the Trinity's divine plan to unfold, a plan that would lead towards the restoration of man's relationship with God.

" God is the greatest general and strategist, Whose strategies no man can replicate. "

As they journeyed out of Egypt toward the desert, Jehovah, now reveal-ing Himself as the loving and caring Father that He is, provided warmth for them at night when it was cold, through a pillar of fire, and shade from the hot desert sun during the day, through a pillar of cloud. What joy must have filled Jehovah to once again have children that He could brood over, provide for, and protect. He could listen to their petition, receive their worship, and have them all to Himself. Not since Adam and Eve in the Garden, did Jehovah have such joy with His children. They were His 'first fruits' after the fall, and, through them, He would call mankind back to their God and Father. His plan for their lives was grand.

Back in Egypt, Pharaoh came out of the palace to face the stench, ruin, and chaos that remained, his head bowed in defeat and shame. Pharaoh had to face the shocking reality that his gods were no gods at all. They were merely the work of man's hands, engineered by Satan to deceive and control all, except the Israelites whose hearts God had kept for Himself. He had to face the fact that all the prayers to the gods of Egypt were use-less and in vain. He and all of Egypt learned the shocking lesson that all of mankind would one day discover—that there is only one true God, Who is the Creator of heaven, earth, and all that are in them.

With the slaves gone and the talk of the superiority of the God of the Jew on the lips of every Egyptian, Pharaoh felt mocked and completely belittled. With an uncontrollable passion for revenge stirring in his heart, he was driven to pursue the slaves and slaughter them once and for all. Jehovah responded by luring him and his mighty army into a fatal trap.

> And it was told the king of Egypt that the people fled: and the heart of Pharaoh and of his servants was turned against the peo-ple, and they said, Why have we done this, that we have let Israel go from serving us?[6] And he made ready his chariot, and took his people with him:[7] And he took six hundred chosen chariots, and all the chariots of Egypt, and captains over every one of them.
>
> —Exodus 14:5–7

The shouts of praise rising from the camp of the Israelites as they rested near the Red Sea, suddenly turned into wails of terror as the thundering sound of horses and chariots filled the air and the realization dawned that Pharaoh's army was in fervent pursuit. God had hedged in His people from all sides. Sandwiched between two mountain ranges to their left and right, and with Pharaoh's charging chariots behind them and the Red Sea before them, they seemed trapped. God had set up an avenue through which He would demonstrate His omnipotence to Pharaoh who dared to challenge Him yet again. Pharaoh and his army, the people of Israel, and the world were about to witness the absolute, undisputable supremacy of Jehovah, and to discover that He is the greatest general and strategist, Whose strategies no man can replicate. Moses cried out to Jehovah who commanded him to stretch out his rod. In obedience to God, Moses stretched his rod over the sea and instantly the waters stood up, leaving a pathway to the Israelites' freedom but serving as a deathtrap for the Egyptians. Jehovah had intervened. He stood between the Egyptian army and the Israelites until they safely crossed the sea. Then He closed up the sea when the Egyptians were in the midst of it killing their entire army. Allow the scriptures to paint the picture of the dramatic unfolding of this awesome event:

> And the LORD said unto Moses, Wherefore criest thou unto me? speak unto the children of Israel, that they go forward:[16] But lift thou up thy rod, and stretch out thine hand over the sea, and divide it: and the children of Israel shall go on dry ground through the midst of the sea.[17] And I, behold, I will harden the hearts of the Egyptians, and they shall follow them: and I will get me honour upon Pharaoh, and upon all his host, upon his chariots, and upon his horsemen.[18] And the Egyptians shall know that I am the LORD, when I have gotten me honour upon Pharaoh, upon his chariots, and upon his horsemen.[19] And the angel of God, which went before the camp of Israel, removed and went behind them; and the pillar of the cloud went from before their face, and stood behind them:[20] And it came between the camp

of the Egyptians and the camp of Israel; and it was a cloud and darkness to them, but it gave light by night to these: so that the one came not near the other all the night.[21] And Moses stretched out his hand over the sea; and the LORD caused the sea to go back by a strong east wind all that night, and made the sea dry land, and the waters were divided.[22] And the children of Israel went into the midst of the sea upon the dry ground: and the waters were a wall unto them on their right hand, and on their left.[23] And the Egyptians pursued, and went in after them to the midst of the sea, even all Pharaoh's horses, his chariots, and his horsemen.[24] And it came to pass, that in the morning watch the LORD looked unto the host of the Egyptians through the pillar of fire and of the cloud, and troubled the host of the Egyptians,[25] And took off their chariot wheels, that they drave them heavily: so that the Egyptians said, Let us flee from the face of Israel; for the LORD fighteth for them against the Egyptians.[26] And the LORD said unto Moses, Stretch out thine hand over the sea, that the waters may come again upon the Egyptians, upon their chariots, and upon their horsemen.[27] And Moses stretched forth his hand over the sea, and the sea returned to his strength when the morning appeared; and the Egyptians fled against it; and the LORD overthrew the Egyptians in the midst of the sea.[28] And the waters returned, and covered the chariots, and the horse-men, and all the host of Pharaoh that came into the sea after them; there remained not so much as one of them.[29] But the children of Israel walked upon dry land in the midst of the sea; and the waters were a wall unto them on their right hand, and on their left.[30] Thus the LORD saved Israel that day out of the hand of the Egyptians; and Israel saw the Egyptians dead upon the sea shore.[31] And Israel saw that great work which the LORD did upon the Egyptians: and the people feared the LORD, and believed the LORD, and his servant Moses.

—Exodus 14:15–31

This undoubtedly was a further demonstration of the astounding power of the God of Israel to serve as a witness of God's supremacy for all generations.

Three months after the Israelites left Egypt, they arrived in Midian and pitched their tents there. Moses went up to Mount Horeb to meet with God and God spoke:

> Thus shalt thou say to the house of Jacob, and tell the children of Israel;[4] Ye have seen what I did unto the Egyptians, and how I bare you on eagles' wings, and brought you unto myself.[5] Now therefore, if ye will obey my voice indeed, and keep my covenant, then ye shall be a peculiar treasure unto me above all people: for all the earth is mine:[6] And ye shall be unto me a kingdom of priests, and an holy nation.
>
> —Exodus 19:3–5

Moses came down from Mount Horeb with instructions from Jehovah to the elders and the rest of the people who agreed to do all that God commanded. This Moses conveyed to God Who then said that He will come down to meet with them after the next three days and further instructed that they should sanctify themselves in preparation for their meeting which would be on the third day.

> And the LORD said unto Moses, Lo, I come unto thee in a thick cloud, that the people may hear when I speak with thee, and believe thee forever. And Moses told the words of the people unto the LORD.[10] And the LORD said unto Moses, Go unto the people, and sanctify them today and tomorrow, and let them wash their clothes,[11] And be ready against the third day: for the third day the LORD will come down in the sight of all the people upon mount Sinai.
>
> —Exodus 19: 9–11

God would not allow the passion of His people to know Him by the sense of sight to interrupt this faith walk which they had embarked upon through their belief in the *Invisible God* for the past 430 years. Therefore, in this meeting, God would conclusively prove to them the reality of His existence and, at the same time, reveal their inability to come together as Father and child. He alone knows that this union must wait until He comes to them in His second dispensation. For now, man must wait as God, in His own way and time, would step into His second dispensation in the Person of God the Son—Jesus. Then, and only then, they would be able to see Him with their natural eyes and touch Him with their hands and relate to Him on a human level.

GOD THE FATHER INTRODUCES HIMSELF TO HIS PEOPLE

We go now to Mount Horeb to witness God's first attempt at fellowshipping with man since the loss of his spiritual birthright and heritage. Unfortunately, this meeting between God and His children could not be like the meetings between God and Adam and Eve. Since the fall of Adam and Eve in the Garden and their separation from God, man had been living out of his natural being. God, who is all Spirit, must now present Himself to His children who are all flesh, a unique reality that only Omniscience can resolve.

Today is the scheduled meeting between God and His children. Moses ascends the mountain and the people gather below, anxiously awaiting their meeting with Jehovah.

> And it came to pass on the third day in the morning, that there were thunders and lightnings, and a thick cloud upon the mount, and the voice of the trumpet exceeding loud; so that all the people that was in the camp trembled.[17] And Moses brought

forth the people out of the camp to meet with God; and they stood at the nether part of the mount.[18] And mount Sinai was altogether on a smoke, because the LORD descended upon it in fire: and the smoke thereof ascended as the smoke of a furnace, and the whole mount quaked greatly.[19] And when the voice of the trumpet sounded long, and waxed louder and louder, Moses spake, and God answered him by a voice.[20] And the LORD came down upon mount Sinai, on the top of the mount: and the LORD called Moses up to the top of the mount; and Moses went up.[21]

And the LORD said unto Moses, Go down, charge the people, lest they break through unto the LORD to gaze, and many of them perish.[22] And let the priests also, which come near to the LORD, sanctify themselves, lest the LORD break forth upon them.[23]

And Moses said unto the LORD, The people cannot come up to mount Sinai: for thou chargedst us, saying, Set bounds about the mount, and sanctify it.[24] And the LORD said unto him, Away, get thee down, and thou shalt come up, thou, and Aaron with thee: but let not the priests and the people break through to come up unto the LORD, lest he break forth upon them.[25] So Moses went down unto the people, and spake unto them.

—Exodus 19:16–25

Herein, the *Invisible God* revealed Himself . . .

And all the people saw the thunderings, and the lightnings, and the noise of the trumpet, and the mountain smoking: and when the people saw it, they removed, and stood afar off.[19] And they

said unto Moses, Speak thou with us, and we will hear: but let
not God speak with us, lest we die.[20] And Moses said unto the
people, Fear not: for God is come to prove you, and that his fear
may be before your faces, that ye sin not.[21] And the people stood
afar off, and Moses drew near unto the thick darkness where
God was.

—Exodus 20:18–21

In this first meeting between Jehovah and His children, they were pet-
rified by His manifested presence, even though what they saw and heard
was just a glimpse of His awesome power and might. They quickly with-
drew, satisfied that they could not enter into His presence.

Jehovah clearly intended this meeting with His children to communicate His love for them and accept their love for Him, but also to let them
know that it was impossible for God and man to have a personal relationship while sin kept them spiritually separated and made them incompat-
ible. This is why God cautioned them twice not to get too close to the
mountain nor touch it since anyone with sin would not survive in His
presence.

This meeting was the mastery of God's wisdom in conditioning
them to receive Him when He would come in His second dispensation
as God the Son—Jesus. In the meantime, they agreed to let Moses be
the intermediary between themselves and God. This was Moses' call and
destiny: to be their deliverer, their prophet, their shepherd, their inter-
cessor, and their advocate. Moses was faithful to that call. Jehovah then
took him to his heavenly reward after they reached Kadeshbarnea where
they looked across the Jordan River and saw the land that He had prepared for His people, the Promised Land. Joshua, Moses' successor, took
them into the land. After Joshua went to his reward, God continued
to raise up prophets, judges, and kings, through whom He spoke and
provided instruction and leadership for His people. This was all part of
His plan to preserve His covenant love-relationship with them and to

reassure them that they would one day be able to relate to Him in a close and intimate way.

" God is not only a master strategist in war,
but also in relationships. "

It was God's heart all along for His people to know of His intentions and plans so that they could live in expectation of His coming and, this time, of His relating to them on a human level.

Throughout the first dispensation of God, as documented in the Old Testament, Jehovah gave prophetic insights, revelation, and utterances to some of His servant-prophets concerning His second dispensation. So too, many of the ordinances and laws in the Old Testament were types and foreshadowings of His coming in the Person of God the Son. Job, Moses, David, Ezekiel, and others received such prophetic insight and revelation and they passed them on to the people and documented them in the Word of God for the benefit of future generations in their quest to know God. The most notable and pointed of these was that of the prophet Isaiah.

> Therefore the Lord himself shall give you a sign; Behold, a virgin shall conceive, and bear a son, and shall call his name Immanuel.
> —Isaiah 7:14

> For unto us a child is born, unto us a son is given: and the government shall be upon his shoulder: and his name shall be called Wonderful, Counsellor, The mighty God, The everlasting Father, The Prince of Peace.
> —Isaiah 9:6

Each prophet that received this revelation lived in the hope that it would happen in his time, but it did not. It was not Jehovah's time, for despite His continuous pleading with Israel to live by His laws they rebelled time and time again. God, above all, understands the nature of fallen man and works through this condition to accomplish His purposes. Sin, acting as a schoolmaster, must finish its work in bringing man to the realization that he cannot live in freedom, happiness, peace, and harmony without God. Thus in the heart of every Jew remained a yearning to have a personal relationship with God.

God is not only a master strategist in war, but also in relationships. God decided to be silent for a season and allow the 'schoolmaster' a free hand to finish his work in them. He knew that if He would hide and be silent once more, they would seek after Him until He responded. Yet, the power of His love seemed to compel Him to bare His sobbing heart to His people before He would go into that period of silence. God chose to illustratively and passionately reveal His woundedness over unfaithful Israel in and through His servant, Hosea the prophet, and, thereafter, commission him to deliver His heart's plea toward his people.

God commands Hosea, the holy prophet to choose Gomer to be his wife. Hosea, yielding himself to God's command, finds her from among the known harlots of that day, a sin-scarred prostitute whose life was marked by wanton pleasures, dissipation and debauchery. Yet, despite her depraved condition, Hosea is able to look beneath the surface decadence and see the beauty buried deep within. Hosea falls passionately in love with Gomer. With that incomprehensible love for her burning in his heart, he takes her off the streets of Jerusalem, cleans her up, decks her off in fine linens and adorns her with jewels. He is a devoted husband; he comforts and protects her and lavishes her with tender care and attention. He treats her with honor and respect, ensuring that as his beloved wife, she wants for nothing. Gomer responds. After a while though, despite her husband's love and loyalty; despite his utter devotion to her; despite her elevated status as his wife with its accompanying comforts and privileges, Gomer begins to thirst again for the perverted thrills and pleasures of her former life and once more craves her many past lovers. Eventually, compelled by her lusts, she turns her back on Hosea's love and, without so much as a backward glance, returns to a life of harlotry. She flaunts herself once more on the streets of Jerusalem as her husband, Hosea, looks on, his deeply wounded heart filled with the pain and anguish of seeing the one he loves being taken advantage of, abused and ill-treated by those who do not care about her, whose motives are selfish and evil and who are incapable of seeing her true value and beauty. He is devastated, for not even she could see what he sees in her. Wracked by disappointment and despair, this eminent prophet, this righteous man, rejected by a harlot, is now the object of derision—mocked and jeered by all. His anger builds as he witnesses his wife, in drunken stupor, take one by one all his valuable love gifts to her and waste them on her other loves. Yet, in spite of Gomer's flagrant infidelity, Hosea fervently loves her still and longs for her to return to him.

In the midst of his grief, miserable and alone, God does the unthinkable. He commissions Hosea to go after Gomer yet again and remarry her in her depraved state. Driven by his unfathomable love, Hosea faithfully goes in search of his estranged, harlot wife. His eyes anxiously search the streets of Jerusalem until finally he sees her broken and disheveled as she stands quivering in the marketplace being auctioned off to the highest bidder. Moved with compassion, he purchases her for fifteen pieces of silver and six and a quarter bushels of barley, the equivalent of the price of a slave and the value of a woman in the fulfillment of a marriage vow. Then, without condemnation or criticism, Hosea scoops Gomer up lovingly in his arms and takes her again to be his bride, once more passionately showering her with his love.

What manner of love is this? A love so relentless; a self-sacrificing love that insists on loving the unlovely; one that pours itself out almost without volition … it is a love that is almost shattering in its purity.

Israel too had turned her back on God and had gone seeking after her many worldly loves instead of responding to God's love which He had so convincingly demonstrated to her. She too had used all that God had given to her in the worship of idols. God used the illustration of Hosea's plight so that His people would be able to relate, on a human level, to the extent of his disappointment and hurt, and grasp the staggering depth of His love for them.

Hosea's matrimonial experience vividly parallels to what God experienced with Israel. God chose this prophet to experience, in the natural, His sobbing heart, after an unfaithful people persisted in going away from Him and further into sin.

Out of the intense pain Hosea experienced, he was able to declare with fidelity God's brokenness over backslidden Israel as God commissioned him to do and, with the utmost conviction, to fervently express God's profound love for His apostate people and His willingness to forgive, welcome, and restore them.

An emphatic Hosea poignantly pleads with Israel, on God's behalf, to come just as they are, decadent and degenerate, back to Him—the One who made them, the One who loves them with an everlasting love and had lovingly nurtured them; the One who longs to have them return to Him and is willing to forgive them, restore them and to re-establish relationship with them just as they are.

Without reserve, God expresses His humanness through Hosea on a level as never before and flagrantly exposes His unconditional love for His people. Israel finally gave in to God's pleadings, repented and returned.

❝Man, having had an experience of God in a personal way, cannot ever be satisfied and fulfilled without Him. ❞

Hosea's love for Gomer is a vivid example to all of us of God's lavish love and relentless pursuit of us. God reveals, through Hosea, His deep passion for us and the extent to which He will go to redeem and restore us to a love relationship with Him. He loves us like no other can; He sees in us the true beauty and value that He placed within us; and no amount of sin and depravation can hide from Him the value that He sees in us.

His is a selfless love, for He gives His all and humbles Himself, laying aside His dignity to redeem us. Just as Gomer was precious to Hosea, so too, we are precious to God and He yearns for us to be reconciled to Him.

It is a proven fact that man, having had an experience of God in a personal way, cannot ever be satisfied and fulfilled without Him. Adam and Eve experienced this and now Israel had discovered it. Yet, God's wisdom necessitated a period of silence between Him and Israel to intensify their yearning for him.

For four hundred years Jehovah remained silent until He was satisfied that Israel was truly remorseful for her ingratitude and dishonor towards Him and, once again, yearned for Him wholeheartedly. After Israel had satisfied her ungodly cravings, she could not find the spiritual fulfillment, security and the love that she had come to know from Jehovah. She fully realized that only in Jehovah could she have complete fulfillment and hope for a blessed eternity.

Israel wanted Jehovah but on a human level and He would oblige them in the process of restoring relationship with them. The work of the school-master and God's silence were accomplishing God's purpose—to reconcile man to God. That process necessitated Jehovah coming to them on their level—the human level—in the Person of God the Son, Jesus, the Second Person in the Trinity.

CHAPTER 7

THE SECOND DISPENSATION: GOD THE SON

THE UNFOLDING OF THE MYSTERY CONTINUES . . .

Love condescends. Omnipotence must step forward and do what only Omnipotence can do, out of His love and for the sake of mankind.

THE FORERUNNER

God now chooses Zechariah, the Jewish high priest during King Herod's reign in Judea, to further advance His plan. Both he and his wife, Elizabeth, are very advanced in years. They are both righteous before God, keeping all the commandments and ordinances, according to the Law of

Moses. At their age, they know that they do not have much time remaining on the earth, and they are troubled that they still have no child to carry on the family name and traditions. For many years, they have been asking God for a son.

" The chosen of God are not exempt from denial, hardships or difficulties. "

In those days, when a woman was without child, it was the common belief that God had closed up her womb as a form of judgment for sin. Bearing that stigma, the woman would withdraw from public life in shame. Elizabeth did the same, but, being a godly woman, while she was in seclusion she spent the time in prayer asking God to grant their wish. Their childless state was by no means God's displeasure. It was His will, unknown to them. God's ways are higher than our ways and His thoughts higher than our thoughts.

As with Zechariah and Elizabeth, the chosen of God are not exempt from denial, hardships, or difficulties. They too must exhibit a level of faith, obedience, and love for God, even in adverse conditions and circumstances, if God chooses to hide Himself and His will from them. It brings pleasure and satisfaction to God when His children, in spite of their trials, continue in the covenant of faith that He made with their forefathers, Abraham, Isaac, and Jacob.

God now sends the Archangel Gabriel to Zechariah with the message that He has heard their prayers and that his wife, Elizabeth, will bear him a son, who they should name John. There would be joy and gladness at his birth and many would rejoice because he would be great in the sight of God. He would be filled with the Holy Ghost while he is still in his mother's womb to enable him to convince Israel to expect the soon coming of the Messiah and to receive God's plan of forgiveness of sins.

Among the many things that the Archangel Gabriel said to Zechariah is that their son John would be the forerunner of God the Son. Further, he tells Zechariah that John would come in the power of the prophet Elijah to turn the hearts of the fathers back to the children and the hearts of the children to their fathers, and to cause the disobedient to turn to the wisdom of the godly. He would prepare God's people for the Lord Jesus, the Christ. Zechariah considered his age and that of his wife, and told Gabriel that this was not possible. Gabriel replied, "Because you do not believe God's Word you would be dumb for a season." Immediately, Zechariah became speechless and remained so until God's Word was fulfilled when John was born. Had Zechariah been allowed to continue to speak he could have easily spoken words of unbelief to Elizabeth, annulled her prayer of faith for a son, and set back God's will, plan, and timing, in His pursuit of restoring man's relationship with Him.

The exceptional nature of John's ministry required divine impetus to succeed, thus he was granted the infilling of the Holy Ghost while he was still in his mother's womb. That would set him apart as a channel for God since the Holy Spirit would have control of his life. His upbringing was in the Judean desert. He was consumed with the things of God and lived a secluded life in prayer, seeking God's leading with regard to his destiny as the forerunner of the Messiah. God gave him the revelation of how to identify the Messiah when He would step forward to begin His ministry of redeeming mankind from their sinful fallen state.

After 400 years of silence, God's voice was heard again echoing in the Judean desert through this fearless prophet. John's voice was like a trumpet—penetrating, soul-searching, and arresting. Everywhere people heard his voice they flocked to see and to listen to him. The people heard God through John's preaching which was passionate, powerful, and convincing. His message was singular and repetitive: The Kingdom of God is at hand! Repent of your sins! Be baptized and get ready to meet the Lord who is soon to be revealed! His message was so powerfully anointed by the Holy Spirit within him that it stirred and awoke the God consciousness in the hearts of the people and many responded to the messenger, the message, and the conviction that gripped their hearts. It would be the dawning of a new day for Israel and for all of mankind since now, through their natural state and senses they would be able to experience God in the flesh. God would do this in the process of leading man back to his spiritual dimension.

John's ministry was unique. He was the prophet that stood between the Old Testament covenant and the New Testament covenant. He was the forerunner for the second dispensation of God the Son—the fulfilling of Isaiah's prophesies.

> Therefore the Lord himself shall give you a sign; Behold, a virgin shall conceive, and bear a son, and shall call his name Immanuel.
> —Isaiah 7:14

God Made Flesh

God now sends His Word, the Second Personality of the Trinity, to take on the form and likeness of man and be the second Adam, to live on the earth as Adam lived and to face the devil and his temptation as Adam did. Remember that Adam was spirit, soul, and body when God created him. As an equal substitute, God is taking upon Himself a human spirit, soul, and body in His quest to redeem mankind and bring man back into sonship, relationship, and eventual dialogue. In choosing this process, the angels in heaven, along with all of God's created beings and creation itself, would see God's justice and continue to reverence Him. This act could only be conceived by Omniscience and Omnipotence; an act that the human intellect cannot formulate, understand or interpret, except by divine revelation from God.

Even as God comes to make Himself known to man through his senses, He still requires man to maintain the covenant of faith which He had established through Abraham in the things unseen and unknown, which are of Him. God expects His people, those who are of the covenant of faith, the spiritual seed of Abraham, to readily accept His acts and ways without demanding proof by sight in order to believe. Conversely, those who are not of the spiritual seed of Abraham would not accept His supernatural acts and ways except they understand them through their senses.

"There can never be more than one God; therefore, the idea of other gods is a fallacy."

To the unbelieving heart, the skeptic, and those who were introduced to a god, or gods, after the order of man's reasoning, I invite you to take a moment to consider who God really is, and must be, and who or what God cannot be. God cannot be anyone or anything or whoever or whatever we think Him or make Him to be. Unless we have the proper concept of God, we would try to equate Him to what we know and understand from our own human, limited perspective. God is not natural; He is supernatural and, unlike man-made gods that are not gods, He can and does perform supernatural acts. Just look around. The world and everything in it is the result of His supernatural acts and how marvelous is His creation! Look at yourself. You are no accident. You are no afterthought. The divine hand of God made you and gave you faculties for love, for relationship, for procreation, for creativity, and more. The very name *God* is reserved for the One who knows all things at all times; the One who is present everywhere at all times and, unlimited in power and ability; the One who is highest in rank and authority. He is divine love, absolute power, complete knowledge and wisdom. He is Sovereign, infallible, and without limitation. He is the One who created every form of life and matter. He is the One who sustains creation and determines the order of all things. God cannot have an origin because He is before all existence. He cannot have any genealogy. This being so, there can never be more than one God; therefore, the idea of other gods is a fallacy. Given the originality and supremacy of God, nothing can reproduce, duplicate, or diminish God.

God is supernatural and everything He does reflects His supernatural character and nature.

Six months after Elizabeth had conceived John the Forerunner, the Archangel Gabriel went to a young virgin by the name of Mary with a message:

> And in the sixth month the angel Gabriel was sent from God unto a city of Galilee, named Nazareth,[27] To a virgin espoused to a man whose name was Joseph, of the house of David; and the virgin's name was Mary.[28] And the angel came in unto her, and said, Hail, thou that art highly favoured, the Lord is with thee: blessed art thou among women.[29] And when she saw him, she was troubled at his saying, and cast in her mind what manner of salutation this should be.[30] And the angel said unto her, Fear not, Mary: for thou hast found favour with God.[31] And, behold, thou shalt conceive in thy womb, and bring forth a son, and shalt call his name JESUS.[32] He shall be great, and shall be called the Son of the Highest: and the Lord God shall give unto him the throne of his father David:[33] And he shall reign over the house of Jacob forever; and of his kingdom there shall be no end.[34] Then said Mary unto the angel, How shall this be, seeing I know not a man?[35] And the angel answered and said unto her, The Holy Ghost shall come upon thee, and the power of the Highest shall overshadow thee: therefore also that holy thing which shall be born of thee shall be called the Son of God.
>
> —Luke 1:26–35

Mary, in faith, received the Word of the Lord:

> And Mary said, Behold the handmaid of the Lord; be it unto me according to thy word.
>
> —Luke 1:38

Many think it unbelievable that a virgin could become pregnant without the involvement of a man. God spoke the world, the moon, stars, galaxies and everything into existence eons ago and they still exist in His perfect order today. Why can He not impregnate a virgin with His divine seed? Is He not the One who made the human body with its organs and functions and determined their responses? Does He not have the right and influence over that which He made? With God, nothing is impossible.

The Angel Gabriel had told Mary that she would bare a child who shall be called "Son of God." It was God's divine wisdom to come to man in the flesh so that He and man could relate to each other on the human level. This was part of His plan in restoring man's relationship with Him.

Man is the object and expression of divine love. God created man for His pleasure and, as His children, to be the heirs of His Kingdom, both in heaven and on earth. Because of the fall, however, every human being came out of Adam and Eve with an inherent nature to sin. Much like Hosea's wife, Gomer, fallen man is in slavery to the sin nature and is unable to free himself from sin. He needs a Redeemer who would pay the price to ransom man from sin and its repercussions, for "the wages of sin is death." The animal sacrifice in the Garden of Eden and throughout the Old Testament was a temporary covering for man's sins—temporary because it was not possible for the blood of animals to take away man's sins as animals are lesser creations than man, who bears the image and likeness of God. No one but God has the qualification and the ability to redeem mankind from his condition. Man's redeemer would have to be a new man—another Adam, born without the sin nature. God, therefore, had to come Himself and He chose to do so through His Word, making it flesh.

Furthermore, in order for the Redeemer to make His entrance into this world, he had to come through a natural birth. However, as a perfect substitute for Adam, he could not be a spirit being but a human being with a sinless nature. A new creation was necessary in man's spiritual recovery because man's seed does not have within it the sinless and divine characteristic for this assignment. Only God has the capacity to produce this new creation.

Should God, in His original divine state, choose to be a substitute for Adam, He would render Himself an unequal substitute because of His supernatural existence when compared with Adam's natural existence. The second Adam must have a natural existence as Adam had. God must therefore place His spiritual seed into a human vessel, which He did in the Virgin Mary, and, through that seed, give natural life to His Word, making Him flesh so He could live among us—a new man, who would bear His divine nature and also bear the nature of the natural man. This would be man's Saviour-Redeemer.

God essentially had two options: He could have left man in his sinful state and under Satan's rule forever, or taken responsibility to be man's redeemer. Love is redemptive. In His love for us, God chose the latter. Thus, God Himself, the Second Person of the Trinity, The Word of God, came and dwelt among us as Jesus Christ, a unique creation: God and man—the Son of God and the Son of Man.

Jesus, this new God-man, would inherit and possess two distinct natures, the divine and the natural, as Adam had. He would be subjected to all the natural temptations as Adam was. He would have a free will as Adam had. He could choose to obey His Father or he could choose to obey Satan. He would be on a mission for His Father to rescue man, redeem him, and bring him back into sonship through His own willing self-sacrifice. He would also fulfill the prophetic declaration which God made to Satan and Adam and Eve in the Garden of Eden when Satan led them into sin—that the "seed of the woman would bruise the serpent's head" (Genesis 3:15)—and bring an end to Satan's rule over mankind and over the earth.

At the birth of Jesus, this new creation, God the Father along with all the host of heaven rejoiced. The angel brought the good news to the shepherds and the host of angels followed with singing and jubilation. What a glorious day it was for heaven and for earth. Since the fall of Adam, the citizens in heaven had been observing and monitoring the events on earth, anxious to see how the redemption of man would come about. Finally, God revealed His plan and they were elated at the greatness and infinite wisdom of God as they began to see and understand God's way of bringing man back to Him.

> [B]ehold, I bring you good tidings of great joy, which shall be to all people.[11] For unto you is born this day in the city of David a Saviour, which is Christ the Lord.[12] And this shall be a sign unto you; Ye shall find the babe wrapped in swaddling clothes, lying in a manger.[13] And suddenly there was with the angel a multitude of the heavenly host praising God, and saying,[14] Glory to God in the highest, and on earth peace, good will toward men.
>
> —Luke 2:10b–14

When Satan found out that Jesus—Emmanuel, the Messiah—was born in Bethlehem, fear gripped his heart the way it did when Moses was born and he again attempted to abort God's plan.

Satan was in a panic. His nightmare had become a reality. Until then, his rule over man and the earth had been uncontested. The earth was his kingdom and he was regarded as the *god of this world*. Now, as had been prophesied, the true King was born and, in time, every king and kingdom must come under His rule and authority. Satan must employ all those under his influence, those seated in high places, to search out and destroy Jesus. He moved upon Herod, who was then king, to seek after Jesus and kill Him. He stirred up religious hatred, passed new laws, and did everything in his power to stop Jesus from stepping into His destiny, but God shielded His new creation—His Son—from Satan's relentless search to find Him and destroy Him.

Despite Satan's every effort, God's divine plan remained on course. Jesus grew up in Nazareth like any other boy, loving and obedient to His parents. Yet, He was different from other boys in that even as a child He was consumed with His Father's business. He was able to hold lengthy discussions about God and the Word of God with the doctors of the Law to their utter amazement. He spoke with knowledge and wisdom and they wondered where He had learned these things. Both Mary, His mother, and Joseph, His adopted father, understanding His divine birth, watched Him closely, and guided Him along their godly traditions.

> Then said Jesus unto them, When ye have lifted up the Son of man, then shall ye know that I am he, and that I do nothing of myself; but as my Father hath taught me, I speak these things.[29]And he that sent me is with me: the Father hath not left me alone; for I do always those things that please him.
>
> —John 8:28–29

> But Jesus answered them, My Father worketh hitherto, and I work.[18] Therefore the Jews sought the more to kill him, because he not only had broken the sabbath, but said also that God was his Father, making himself equal with God.[19] Then answered Jesus and said unto them, Verily, verily, I say unto you, The Son can do nothing of himself, but what he seeth the Father do: for what things soever he doeth, these also doeth the Son likewise.[20] For the Father loveth the Son, and sheweth him all things that himself doeth: and he will shew him greater works than these, that ye may marvel.[21] For as the Father raiseth up the dead, and quickeneth them; even so the Son quickeneth whom he will.[22]For the Father judgeth no man, but hath committed all judgment unto the Son:
>
> —John 5:17–22

> Verily, verily, I say unto you, The hour is coming, and now is, when the dead shall hear the voice of the Son of God: and they that hear shall live.[26] For as the Father hath life in himself; so hath he given to the Son to have life in himself;[27] And hath given him authority to execute judgment also, because he is the Son of man.
>
> —John 5:25–27

Even as Jesus matured, increasing in knowledge and wisdom through His relationship with His Father, Jehovah was instructing John the Baptist, Jesus' Forerunner, to institute the ordinance of water baptism as a public confession of their faith and acceptance of the coming Savior. Baptism was also a sign that would mark the transition between the dispensations of the Old Testament covenant enacted through the Law of Moses and the New Testament covenant of grace and forgiveness of sins through the blood of Jesus.

Now the time that God had set for man's redemption had come, and John the Baptist was the one ordained by God to give that revelation by which to identify man's Savior to Israel and the world.

> He (Jesus) it is, who coming after me is preferred before me, whose shoe's latchet I am not worthy to unloose.[28] These things were done in Bethabara beyond Jordan, where John was baptizing.[29] The next day John seeth Jesus coming unto him, and saith, Behold the Lamb of God, which taketh away the sin of the world.[30] This is he of whom I said, After me cometh a man which is preferred before me: for he was before me.[31] And I knew him not: but that he should be made manifest to Israel, therefore am I come baptizing with water.[32] And John bare record, saying, I saw the Spirit descending from heaven like a dove, and it abode upon him.[33] And I knew him not: but he that sent me to baptize with water, the same said unto me, Upon whom thou shalt see the Spirit descending, and remaining on him, the same is he which baptizeth with the Holy Ghost.[34] And I saw, and bare record that this is the Son of God.
>
> —John 1:27–34

Crowds of people flocked the River Jordan in response to John the Baptist's preaching, repenting of their sins and were baptized. Without fanfare, Jesus appeared on the scene and, without a word, He walked past the crowd and stood before John to be baptized of Him. Although John and

Jesus were first cousins, they had never met, but, at the day of their meeting, there was no doubt about who they were to each other. John spoke first, aptly so, as Jesus' forerunner, announcer and identifier of the Messiah to Israel. Consumed by the visible appearance of Jesus, with passion and relief John shouted so that the large gathering could hear, "Behold, the Lamb of God which takes away the sin of the world." John, knowing that Jesus had no sin to confess and to declare publicly, could not understand why Jesus would want to be baptized. John said, "I have need to be baptized of Thee, and comest thou to me?" Jesus immediately answered him saying that He was doing this to fulfill all righteousness as an example for all men to follow, in order to satisfy God's new requirement of obedience. Then John baptized Him and, as he was doing so, God spoke audibly from heaven saying, "This is my beloved Son in whom I am well pleased." Simultaneously, the Spirit of God, like a dove, came and lighted on Jesus, confirming His identity to John (Matthew 3:1-17).

Here is an instance when the Trinity is identified simultaneously, to give witness and testimony that they are united in the pursuit of man's redemption.

What a day of revelation for John and for Israel. Messiah-Savior had finally come to give His life sacrificially as the Lamb of God, to pay the penalty for man's sin and to redeem mankind. John was given to know and understand Jesus and His ministry on the earth and so precise was his interpretation when he said that Jesus came to take away the *sin* of the world, referring to the sin nature in man.

What a glorious plan and cooperation by the Trinity to redeem man! What a demonstration of love for mankind! God condescended to rescue man. Love is on display and the Trinity gave witness to the world that all might know and respond.

The moment of heaven's anticipation had come. The Word, sent by the Father, had become flesh and now He was about to step into the first phase of His mission, empowered by the Holy Spirit.

As Jesus stepped out of the River Jordan, the Spirit of God led him into the wilderness to subject Him to Satan's temptation. This was a necessary step because Adam and Eve had been subjected to Satan in the Garden of Eden when they fell. Jesus, the second Adam, took up the mantle at the exact point that Adam and Eve had left off. The temptation had to take place in the wilderness, where there would be no one to give support to Jesus when Satan, using his skill of deception, makes his bid to capture Jesus' will. In fact, the temptation of Jesus would even be greater than Adam's because He did not have a companion to support Him, nor did He have food and water to aid Him, nor the beauty and comfort of paradise as Adam had. Jesus had only the hot, rough, dry, and barren desert, unfit for human survival. The location and conditions were arranged by God, His Father, and the stage was set for the showdown between Satan and Jesus, Who came to pick up where Adam fell.

Satan, knowing that Jesus was the Son of God, and realizing that it would not be easy to deceive the second Adam as he did the first Adam, waited for Jesus' most vulnerable moment, when He had not eaten or drunk for forty days and forty nights and was weak from hunger and thirst. Remember that Jesus had a dual nature, a divine nature and a human nature, and He could draw from either nature as He desired. If, in this contest, He draws from His divine nature He would immediately disqualify Himself as a fair substitute for the first Adam, and Satan would have won the legal right to victory by heaven's just law. For this reason, Jesus had to stay within His human nature. Satan therefore had the greater advantage as a supernatural being over Jesus in the flesh. These were the terms under which the contest in the Garden of Eden with Adam has been carried out and so, this is exactly how it must now be allowed. God is fair and just. Additionally, Satan does not need food and water for his energy and survival, but Jesus does.

Satan was confident that in Jesus' weakened condition, He would welcome some bread to strengthen Him for the contest. Satan knew he would have to employ a more devious strategy from the one that he used in the garden, so he was careful to steer away from offering bread to Jesus but he tempted Him instead to make bread out of stones. Satan's scheme this time was to have Jesus step out of His humanity into His divinity. If Jesus had done as Satan had suggested, He would have deviated from the will and purpose of His Father, giving His will over to Satan. Satan would then have gained access to Jesus' spirit and would have been able to corrupt His sinless nature as he had done with Adam and Eve. Moreover, Satan could claim victory by default had Jesus acted out of His divinity and thus rendered Himself an unsuitable substitute for Adam.

Jesus' hunger was real. His physically weakened state was real, but to Him, His Father's Word was even more real. He knew that His Father's words are Spirit—they are life-giving and life-sustaining—and would provide Him with all the physical energy He needed.

Jesus rejected outright Satan's seemingly grand suggestion for Him to feed Himself. Jesus' response must have struck Satan as a bolt of lightning when He replied, "It is written, man shall not live by bread alone, but by every word that proceedeth out of the mouth of God." Satan, to mask his shock and keep his composure, makes another appeal, and another, and another, but with every attempt, Jesus' response is the same, "It is written . . . It is written . . .," which is to say, "My Father said . . . My Father said . . . ."

Adam and Eve fell at Satan's very first temptation. However, Jesus, though He faced three major, cleverly designed and well-timed temptations, confounded Satan at each of his cunning attempts. Satan realized that he could not break through Jesus' line of defense so he left Him for a season hoping to try again at future times. Jesus won the contest and battle convincingly, with no struggle whatsoever, by taking sides with His Father and being loyal to His Word. This is the biblical account of Jesus' temptations:

> Then was Jesus led up of the Spirit into the wilderness to be tempted of the devil.[2] And when he had fasted forty days and forty nights, he was afterward an hungred.[3] And when the tempter came to him, he said, If thou be the Son of God, command that these stones be made bread.[4] But he answered and

said, It is written, Man shall not live by bread alone, but by every word that proceedeth out of the mouth of God.[5] Then the devil taketh him up into the holy city, and setteth him on a pinnacle of the temple,[6] And saith unto him, If thou be the Son of God, cast thyself down: for it is written, He shall give his angels charge concerning thee: and in their hands they shall bear thee up, lest at any time thou dash thy foot against a stone.[7] Jesus said unto him, It is written again, Thou shalt not tempt the Lord thy God.[8] Again, the devil taketh him up into an exceeding high mountain, and sheweth him all the kingdoms of the world, and the glory of them;[9] And saith unto him, All these things will I give thee, if thou wilt fall down and worship me.[10] Then saith Jesus unto him, Get thee hence, Satan: for it is written, Thou shalt worship the Lord thy God, and him only shalt thou serve.[11] Then the devil leaveth him, and, behold, angels came and ministered unto him.

—Matthew 4:1–11

And when the devil had ended all the temptation, he departed from him for a season.[14] And Jesus returned in the power of the Spirit into Galilee: and there went out a fame of him through all the region round about.[15] And he taught in their synagogues, being glorified of all.

—Luke 4:13–15

This was the beginning of a new round of victories for God and all of mankind leading up to man's spiritual restoration and relationship with God. This was also the beginning of a new round of defeat of Satan.

During Jesus' ministry on the earth, He taught His disciples that the key to success and victory is to live by His Word and because He and His Father are one, His word is His Father's Word. Jesus taught His disciples all the principles of the Kingdom of God and Heaven and demonstrated through many miracles that He was indeed the expected Messiah. He taught them how to live the abundant life, the highest quality of life that can be lived on the earth.

" *Love for God, absolute faith in Him, and loyalty and obedience to His word are prerequisites to living in the spiritual dimension.* **"**

Jesus' life communicated to His followers the fact of His dual nature. His teachings to His disciples were designed to awaken them to a new order of living which was to give emphasis to the spiritual dimension and which would be manifested through them when they live by His word. Their love for Him, their absolute faith in Him and their loyalty and obedience to His word would be prerequisites to living in the spiritual dimension.

Nicodemus, a Jewish high priest had been observing Jesus and came to Him to inquire about His supernatural ability to work miracles. Nicodemus, together with Jesus' disciples, received the revelation of how man would be able to regain access into the Kingdom of Heaven.

> There was a man of the Pharisees, named Nicodemus, a ruler of the Jews:[2] The same came to Jesus by night, and said unto him, Rabbi, we know that thou art a teacher come from God: for no man can do these miracles that thou doest, except God be with him.[3] Jesus answered and said unto him, Verily, verily, I say unto thee, Except a man be born again, he cannot see the kingdom of God.[4] Nicodemus saith unto him, How can a man be born when he is old? can he enter the second time into his mother's womb, and be born?[5] Jesus answered, Verily, verily, I say unto thee, Except a man be born of water and of the Spirit, he cannot enter into the kingdom of God.[6] That which is born of the flesh is flesh; and that which is born of the Spirit is spirit.[7] Marvel not

that I said unto thee, Ye must be born again.[8] The wind bloweth where it listeth, and thou hearest the sound thereof, but canst not tell whence it cometh, and whither it goeth: so is every one that is born of the Spirit.

—John 3:1–8

Non-Christians have been struggling with the idea as well as the reason for the *new birth,* but logical thinking would point to the fact that every human being gained access into the natural world through the process of a *natural birth.* It is therefore only practical and absolutely necessary to have a spiritual birth in order to gain entrance into the spiritual Kingdom of Heaven. Heaven is a spiritual domain, and man in his fleshly state cannot enter into it, but his spirit can if it has been redeemed from sin by accepting Jesus Christ as Savior and Lord. Like Nicodemus, it would be prudent to accept this revelation and secure the right of entrance into the Kingdom of Heaven.

Jesus Christ's ministry on the earth lasted for three and a half years. It culminated in His death on the cross where He paid the ultimate redemption price by the shedding of His sinless blood to make atonement for the sin of mankind. Through His sacrifice, Jesus also made available to man the spirit-to-Spirit reconnection to God—direct, personal access to Almighty God, freely and without works.

The loss of man's access to the spiritual realm and to God was symbolized by a thick veil that separated the Holy of Holies from the outer court in the Jewish Temple. The Holy of Holies was an area which housed the Ark the Covenant where the Presence of God was resident, an area to which only the consecrated high priest had access. All else, including the other priests, conducted their observances in the outer court. It was in this outer court the people came to make their blood sacrifices as a temporary atonement for their sin as God had instructed them to do in the old covenant. This was a foreshadowing of the death of Jesus, the sacrificial Lamb of God. When Jesus died on the cross, simultaneously, this huge veil in the Jewish Temple of worship was torn from top to bottom by unseen angelic hands. This signaled to all that Jesus was God's ultimate 'High Priest'. There was no longer a need for a priest to act as an intermediary between God and man and to make temporary atonement for sin. Through the sacrifice of Jesus' sinless life and his shed blood the atonement for the sin of all mankind was fully accomplished and available to those who would confess their sins and receive Jesus Christ as their personal Savior and Lord. The wages of sin were paid in full. Jesus' death, therefore, was a major achievement toward reconciling man to God.

There was additional significance to the death and burial of Jesus Christ, as we shall see. The spirits of all the righteous who had died before Jesus Christ came to earth to save man from his sins were sent to a place beneath the earth called *Sheol,* to wait for the Lord's coming. This was a place where both the righteous and the wicked went, separated into respective compartments. The faith of the righteous in God gave hope in the promised Redeemer who would deliver them from *Sheol* at Jesus' resurrection from the dead. He would accompany them to their permanent home in heaven. Men like Job, David and others embraced and proclaimed this hope. On the other hand, the spirits of all the unrighteous who had died were ushered to *Gehenna,* a place of torment, as punishment for rejecting God's prescribed law (Luke 16: 19-31).

The three days Jesus spent in the grave served to accomplish some important tasks of His mission: firstly, to make an unannounced visit to Satan in his underground kingdom of darkness where he has his headquarters, and secondly, to release the righteous souls who were waiting in *Sheol* for His appearance and for their redemption.

When Satan had Jesus crucified and buried, he thought he had defeated Him. He did not know that he had been lured into an entrapment and, by heaven's law, brought about his own sentencing for banishment into the Lake of Fire for committing treason and murder. Jesus' death and burial released His spirit from His body and gave Him access into the underworld. Jesus was now at liberty to enter hell to keep His last appointment with Satan.

Convinced that he had defeated Jesus, Satan decided to have a victory celebration. It was to be the celebration of celebrations. Using one's imagination, one can surmise that he must have summoned all his demons (fallen angels) from all over the earth that had supported him in his abuse of mankind and in the death of Jesus Christ. After all, this was his day for glory. With pride, Satan would have taken his seat upon his throne, reminiscing over his struggle on the earth with the second Adam, and recalling the times when he thought that he might not have been able to prevail against Jesus and how close he came to being defeated by Him. He shuddered at the thought of being banished by God into the Lake of Fire that God had prepared for him and his demons.

Let us take an imaginative journey to that hellish event. Picture hell's victory party in progress: never was there greater reveling among the demons. They were engaged in wild orgies and other forms of perversion and debauchery. Hell is in its hellish glory. A constant flow of high-ranking demons approach Satan's throne bowing down before him proclaiming, "Long live Satan, long live Satan!" At the end of this long procession, Satan rises from his elevated seat and pompously waves his hand, immediately gaining the attention of all present. As he begins to speak in response to all the acclamation given him, a thunderous satanic laughter erupts from his gruesome mouth and, beating his chest with his fist in triumph, Satan proudly proclaims, "I am now officially god and lord of the earth!"

The crowd of demons responds in an uproar of exuberant acknowledgement. Satan continues his rhetoric saying, "We were not allowed in heaven to overthrow Him. He was too powerful; but on earth in the form of a mere man . . ." An explosion of riotous laughter interrupts his speech. Satan interjects, "On the earth He escaped us for a while because of His uncompromising stand on Jehovah's Word, and there were times that I actually began to think that He might win again. Finally, we were able to close in on Him and set the perfect trap through the religious leaders. That is when we got Judas, one of His trusted disciples, to turn against Him; I knew then, that we had Him!" The demons cannot contain themselves as their jubilation climaxes to a wild frenzy. Satan then pays homage to those that were instrumental in bringing him the victory, and with much pomp and ceremony, awards and crowns are presented to specially signaled-out demons such as religion, lies, slander, gossip, hatred, jealousy and others.

While hell's party was is progress, Jesus spends two days surveying other regions of hell, noting the ravages that sin, death, and the grave had brought upon mankind. He looks upon the tortured souls in hell with grief and sorrow. When they see Him, they plead with Him to give them another chance, promising to live for God and their fellow man. They promise to go to their loved ones and tell them about the reality of hell, to tell them about Satan's deception and lies, of his enticements and entrapments through ungodly living, selfishness, unfaithfulness, pride, and other ungodly negative traits; but it is too late.

His visit to *Sheol,* however, is far different. The first to recognize Him is Abraham who breaks out in rejoicing, followed by the other righteous saints. Jesus speaks to them for a while and informs them that He would be back tomorrow.

Today is the third day. Hell is rocking with the rhythm of earth's music and the demons are in a lewd, sick frenzy, unbothered by the filth and slime that have piled up over the past two days of hellish glory. Satan is seated on his throne intoxicated by the glory he is receiving.

In the midst of the wild madness, a gluttonous demon that was busy gorging himself with an assortment of food and drink suddenly freezes. He sees what looks like a light flickering in the distance. A nearby demon, noticing his strange demeanor, asks him what is the matter but unable to speak, he simply points a gnarled finger. After a long silence, he finally stammers out the words: "I-I-I t-thought I-I saw a l-light!" Almost instantly, another demon confirms in a panic, "There is a light in the distance. What could it be? How is it possible?" One by one, the demons begin to notice. Stunned and confused, they stare in stupefied silence at the tiny speck of light way off in the black abyss. As the light begins to grow and take form, the realization of its significance dawns. Then, out of the silence a faint demonic scream is heard, then another, then yet another, until all of hell erupts in a crazed panic as the light grows closer and closer, getting bigger and brighter as it approaches Satan's throne. A crescendo of bloodcurdling screams now fills the dark expanse of hell and terror prevails. The wild party comes to an abrupt halt; demons begin to scamper in all directions as they try to flee from the brightness of the light. One of Satan's chief demons shouts over the raucous noise, "It is Adam, the second Adam! He is the Light!" Another says, "It is Jehovah!" And another chimes in, "It is the glory of Jehovah!" Satan, paralyzed with apprehension, is glued to his throne, confused, deranged and in total shock. His entire body now vibrates uncontrollably, and using his forearm as a shield, tries in vain not to look upon the glory of the Son of God approaching him. Jesus, the Mighty Conqueror, with absolute authority, approaches Satan's throne, and standing at arm's length from Satan, stares at him fixedly. Satan, unable to bear His overpowering presence, drops to his knees and bows low at the feet of Jesus. Jesus orders him to stand but his knees buckle and he stumbles and falls. Two unsteady demons at his side assist him to his feet; he stands slumped in total defeat, his head hanging low. Jesus declares to him, "I have come for the keys— the keys of the kingdom of this world which you stole from Adam." Jesus' eyes rest upon a thick cord around Satan's waist upon which hangs a large golden key. Satan quickly tries to turn his body to conceal it but before he can, Jesus with one swift sweep of His hand yanks the key off the cord, turns His back, and walks off. As He goes, demons all along the way fall prostrate upon their faces, some so still as if dead. As Jesus starts to ascend out of that region of hell Satan appears behind him and stretches out his hands towards Him as though to lay hold of Him, but Jesus without look-ing back, slams His heel unto Satan's head. He falls to the ground in a roar of excruciating pain, his voice drowning out all the other horrid sounds of hell. As Jesus walks away, the glory that emanates from Him illuminates the way. He places the key into the lock on an iron-looking door and opens it. The occupants of *Sheol* follow Jesus praising joyfully as they ascend with Him out of the bowels of the earth. Adam and Eve, Job, Noah, Abraham, Isaac, Jacob, and thousands of souls resurrect with their Lord. They dis-perse in groups throughout the Holy City and many see them.

Jesus, when he had cried again with a loud voice, yielded up the ghost.[51] And, behold, the veil of the temple was rent in twain from the top to the bottom; and the earth did quake, and the rocks rent;[52] And the graves were opened; and many bodies of the saints which slept arose,[53] And came out of the graves after his resurrection, and went into the holy city, and appeared unto many.

—Matthew 27:50–53

Through the voluntary death of Jesus Christ, His burial and resurrection from the dead, He provided redemption for all of mankind, paying the penalty for our sin that we inherited from Adam. Now, through Him we have access to the Father when we repent of our sins, and by faith receive Him into our heart as our Savior and Lord. God loves man so much and we mean so much to Him, that He condescended by sending His Word to take on the lower creation of man in order to redeem him and bring him back into relationship, fellowship, and dialogue.

For God so loved the world, that he gave his only begotten Son, that whosoever believeth in him should not perish, but have everlasting life.

—John 3:16

For by grace are ye saved through faith; and that not of yourselves: it is the gift of God:[9] Not of works, lest any man should boast.

—Ephesians 2:8–9

Religious acts were never God's requirement to remove man's sins and bring him back to God. God's law says that without the shedding of blood (sinless blood), there is no remission of sin and Jesus was the only man who qualified.

CHAPTER 8

JESUS, SON OF GOD– SON OF MAN

The distinction, Son of God–Son of Man, has puzzled the wise and prudent, the skeptic, the atheist, and the doubters of God in every generation. They find it convenient to question God's ability to make a new creation of man who would have a dual nature, that of God and man—the divine and the natural. Yet, a careful study of the Word of God on the life of Jesus Christ gives a clear depiction of this distinction.

Let us look again at His birth. Was the seed that gave conception to Jesus Christ a human seed or a divine seed? Did Joseph's seed impregnate the virgin, Mary, or did God?

To answer these questions, let us recall Isaiah's prophesy given some 734 years before the birth of Jesus Christ. Herein, Isaiah, under prophetic unction of God, declared the birth of 'a son' whose name, among others, would be 'the almighty God, the everlasting Father'. God was destined to come as Jesus 'the son' but further to this, it was declared that the Lord Himself will perform this miraculous feat—making this child of divine conception.

For unto us a child is born, unto us a son is given: and the government shall be upon his shoulder: and his name shall be called Wonderful, Counsellor, The mighty God, The everlasting Father, The Prince of Peace.[7] Of the increase of his government and peace there shall be no end, upon the throne of David, and upon his kingdom, to order it, and to establish it with judgment and with justice from henceforth even for ever. **The zeal of the LORD of hosts will perform this**.

—Isaiah 9:6–7 (bold print for emphasis)

Isaiah, continuing, under the prophetic unction of God, and speaking again of the same event of the coming of the Messiah–Son of God, said,

And there shall come forth a rod out of the stem of Jesse, and a Branch shall grow out of his roots:[2]

—Isaiah 11:1

This alludes to the fact of human involvement and of an earthly genealogy in Jesse, the father of King David from whose line came Jacob the father of Joseph, the eventual husband of Mary of whom was born Jesus the Messiah-Savior (Matthew: 1-16).

The account surrounding Mary's pregnancy was the fulfillment of Isaiah's prophetic writings. So, was the seed that gave conception to Jesus Christ therefore, a human seed or a divine seed? Did Joseph's seed impregnate the Virgin Mary or did God? The conclusion is obvious and undeniable. It was indeed a divine seed that impregnated Mary. God performed it and simply enlisted the involvement of the human factor—Mary's womb. Mary herself was puzzled when it was announced by the Angel Gabriel that she was chosen as the human vessel to give the Word of God his natural birth. She asked him, how can this be and how is this possible? Her question was in line with human impossibilities. Joseph, to whom she was espoused at the time, also had to deal with the fact of her pregnancy until Gabriel assured him that it was God's doing and he accepted it.

Again we must, at all times, keep in mind the right concept of God as "All-Mighty" and "Omnipotent" for as the Angel Gabriel said to Mary in answer to her question, "with God nothing shall be impossible."

You will recall that before the incarnation, Jesus pre-existed and co-existed in heaven as the Word. The Trinity—Father, Son, and Holy Ghost—was identified in Genesis as co-existent and co-equal. According to the Apostle John's revelation:

> In the beginning was the Word, and the Word was with God, and the Word was God.[2] The same was in the beginning with God.[3] All things were made by him; and without him was not anything made that was made.[4] In him was life; and the life was the light of men.
>
> —John 1:1–4

> He was in the world, and the world was made by him, and the world knew him not.[11] He came unto his own, and his own received him not.[12] But as many as received him, to them gave he power to become the sons of God, even to them that believe on his name:[13] Which were born, not of blood, nor of the will of the flesh, nor of the will of man, but of God.[14] And the Word was made flesh, and dwelt among us, (and we beheld his glory, the glory as of the only begotten of the Father,) full of grace and truth.
>
> —John 1:10–14

Let us also remember that the three personalities of the Trinity continue to cooperate with each other in the plan of restoration of mankind. John 1:1 confirms the distinction of Persons within the Godhead but there was never a time when the Godhead was ever separated. Each Person in the Godhead was allowed prominence in Their dispensation while the other Persons gave Their support silently in accomplishing Their united purpose of redeeming man.

Through the incarnation, the Word became flesh. This incarnation was appointed by God the Father, personified in God the Son and executed through God the Holy Spirit, Who impregnated Mary with a new seed, the only one of its kind—Divine, yet with all the characteristics of a human being. The seed was not a copy or duplicate of another seed. It was a new creation—an original. The first Adam was original and the second Adam had to be original. It had never happened before but was destined to produce after its kind in the miracle of the new birth which was introduced to Nicodemus by Jesus. (John 3:1-8)

> **"***It is the arrogance of man's fallen nature to think that Almighty God cannot do what man cannot do.* **"**

Adam was not born of a Divine Seed. He was not born out of conception. He was a new creation—an original. He was never a baby and therefore did not grow up into adulthood. He was born of the Breath of God—the Life-giving Spirit—and a natural seed was placed within him to produce after his kind. Adam's being was a miracle as Christ's being was a miracle.

To God, this is a simple act—a creative miracle; to man it seems impossible. It is the arrogance of man's fallen nature to think that Omnipotence, Almighty God, cannot do what he (man) cannot do.

Jesus' incarnation was unique—God and Man in one—the Son of God and the Son of Man. This super-human could operate out of His divine nature or out of His human nature as He wills; but throughout His life on earth, He never compromised the two natures. To do justice to the biblical data concerning Christ, one must hold fast to two important strands of truth about Christ. First, there is the reality of His two natures; and second, that He maintained the integrity of these two natures—that is, Jesus did not draw upon his human nature when dealing with spiritual things nor did He draw upon His divinity when dealing with natural things, thereby maintaining the unmingled union of these two natures. From boyhood to His ascension, Jesus exhibited, at all times, the full nature and characteristics (fruit of the spirit) that expressed the reality of the spiritual life within Him and which identifies the divine life, and thus differentiates it from the natural life. In the book of Luke, chapter two, we see Jesus at the tender age of twelve in the temple speaking with a level of knowledge and understanding far beyond His years as He engaged in a spiritual discussion with the PhDs of the Law—the doctors of religion who were the assigned authority on the Word of God. How was this possible? With the divine life inherent in Jesus, expression of that life came naturally because whatever is inherent in us expresses itself without tutoring, although tutoring helps to develop what is inherent. Without coercion, His spirit craved relationship with God; therefore, when He went to the temple in Jerusalem with His parents to celebrate the Passover feast, all that He saw and all that He heard stirred that inherent divine life and He spontaneously asked questions of the doctors of the Law.

> And it came to pass, that after three days they found him in the temple, sitting in the midst of the doctors, both hearing them, and asking them questions.[47] And all that heard him were astonished at his understanding and answers.
>
> —Luke 2:46–47

On the other hand, Jesus displayed all the characteristics of an earthly child. As a baby, Jesus cried when He wanted the attention of His mother, and when He was hungry, He ate. He had feelings—earthly feelings. He wept. He expressed compassion and He rested when He was tired. These are all characteristics of the natural man.

Jesus was full deity and full humanity—Son of God–Son of Man!

To be on a divine mission, He had to be divinely empowered. To be on an earthly mission, He had to be appointed and empowered by the Spirit of God—The Holy Spirit—on earth. The success of His mission hung upon these two facts. Recognizing and accepting the fact of His dual nature is essential in understanding His life and in understanding His mission. As Son of Man, He needed a boat to cross the Sea of Galilee. As Son of God, He walked on the Sea of Galilee. As Son of God, heaven was His home. However, while Jesus was the Son of Man, earth was his domain during His mission. He said to the opposing religious leaders who were always trying to trap Him with man-made doctrines: "I am in the world, but I am not of the world."

> Ye are from beneath; I am from above: ye are of this world; I am not of this world.
>
> —John 8:23

As Son of Man, He was crucified, nailed to a cross, killed, and buried; but before it all happened He said, "On the third day I would rise again." In addition, "No man has the power to take my life, but I have the power to lay it down and I have the power to pick it up again." Why did Jesus say this? It is because He was God and man at the same time. As Son of God, He ascended into heaven when His work was finished. Many witnessed His ascension, including two angels whose purpose was to assure the disciples that one day Jesus would return to earth in the same manner as they saw Him leave.

> [H]e was taken up; and a cloud received him out of their sight.[10] And while they looked stedfastly toward heaven as he went up, behold, two men stood by them in white apparel;[11] Which also said, Ye men of Galilee, why stand ye gazing up into heaven? this same Jesus, which is taken up from you into heaven, shall so come in like manner as ye have seen him go into heaven.
>
> —Acts 1:9b–11

Jesus is God in the flesh. The Bible says the fullness of God dwelt in Him bodily. He was in the Father and the Father was in Him. He was in the Holy Ghost and the Holy Ghost was in Him. They were inseparable.

He was the firstborn of the new creation—Son of God. When an individual repents of his sin and accepts Jesus as his Savior and Lord, he experiences the miracle of the new birth through the impartation of the spiritual seed of Christ into his heart. He too is now a new creation, after the order of Jesus Christ, with the potential to become a son of God by feeding and nourishing his spirit with the written Word of God and giving it first place in his life. He is also now empowered by the Holy Spirit as Jesus was. Those who do so become the true followers of Jesus Christ and partakers of His divine nature. Man's spiritual walk has just begun.

CHAPTER 9

THE THIRD DISPENSATION: GOD THE HOLY SPIRIT

THE UNFOLDING OF THE MYSTERY CULMINATES . . .

Jesus had accomplished His mission. He paid the penalty for man's sin and provided a way for man to be reconciled to the Father. He took the keys of death and hell from Satan and broke sin's dominion. Man no longer has to live a life enslaved by sin and restricted by his natural senses. If man so chooses, he can accept God's offer of redemption through Jesus Christ, be liberated from the power of sin through the experience of the new birth. Man can then live as God had always intended for him to live and maintain a personal relationship with Him.

Yet, that is but the beginning of the new life. The disciples knew that only too well. For three and a half years they had walked with Jesus, had listened to His teachings, had experienced the comfort and assurance of His physical presence, and had witnessed His power. Now Jesus was preparing to return to heaven where He and His Father would reunite. Understandably, the disciples were filled with apprehension and sorrow at the thought of losing Him. What was more, Jesus had entrusted them with a great commission:

> [19] Go ye therefore, and teach all nations, baptizing them in the name of the Father, and of the Son, and of the Holy Ghost: [20] Teaching them to observe all things whatsoever I have commanded you: and, lo, I am with you always, even unto the end of the world.
>
> ——Matthew 28:19–20.

How could they possibly accomplish this monumental task and continue their journey without Him? Why would Jesus leave them now, knowing that persecution and conflict awaited them? He had been their shield, their power and their wisdom—their all. The hierarchy of Judaism had been able to successfully plot against Jesus. They had worked through hatred and lies, using false witnesses to instigate His brutal beating, His death and crucifixion. If the Jewish religious leaders had succeeded in killing Jesus, what chance would his disciples have against them? They wondered whether they even had the will to carry on in the ministry He had entrusted to them.

After all, they knew that they had failed Him many times in the past. When He had expected them to support Him in prayer as He faced the reality of impending crucifixion, they had fallen asleep. Even in His darkest hour, when one might expect His followers to stand with Him as He faced arrest, vicious beatings, and incomparable sufferings, they had fled in fear of their lives. Peter, in particular, knew too well the disgrace of not only having abandoned Jesus, but of having three times denied even knowing "the man," as he put it. Despite his earlier self-confident professions of faithfulness and loyalty to Jesus, at the moment of crisis, he rejected even a hint of any association with Jesus, not even referring to Him by name.

His usual words of bravado and boldness had abandoned him when put to the test.

It is no wonder the disciples felt little hope of survival and that fear had begun to grip their hearts. Jesus, knowing their inabilities, had given them promises and assurances for their continuance and success in carrying on His ministry.

The most notable of the promises was that on His return to the Father, He would ask Him to send the Holy Spirit in His place to help them keep His teachings and accomplish His commission:

> If ye love me, keep my commandments.[16] And I will pray the Father, and he shall give you another Comforter, that he may abide with you for ever;[17] Even the Spirit of truth; whom the world cannot receive, because it seeth him not, neither knoweth him: but ye know him; for he dwelleth with you, and shall be in you.[18] I will not leave you comfortless: I will come to you.[19] Yet a little while, and the world seeth me no more; but ye see me: because I live, ye shall live also.[20] At that day ye shall know that I am in my Father, and ye in me, and I in you.[21] He that hath my commandments, and keepeth them, he it is that loveth me: and he that loveth me shall be loved of my Father, and I will love him, and will manifest myself to him.[22] Judas saith unto him, not Iscariot, Lord, how is it that thou wilt manifest thyself unto us, and not unto the world?[23] Jesus answered and said unto him, If a man love me, he will keep my words: and my Father will love him, and we will come unto him, and make our abode with him.[24] He that loveth me not keepeth not my sayings: and the word which ye hear is not mine, but the Father's which sent me.[25] These things have I spoken unto you, being yet present with you.[26] But the Comforter, which is the Holy Ghost, whom the Father will send in my name, he shall teach you all things, and bring all things to your remembrance, whatsoever I have said unto you.
>
> —John 14:15-26

Although they may have been somewhat reassured by Jesus' promises they probably did not understand fully what He meant. Who was this "Comforter" and how would they know him? What did Jesus mean when He said that He would be "in them," and they "in Him"?

We must be reminded that all that God does is guided by purpose and objective, and with eternity in mind. Jesus' departure from the earth was all part of the Trinity's perfect and ingenious plan.

The Trinity's plan to restore man to intimacy with God would now come into sharper focus with the coming of the Holy Spirit. The Trinity foreknew that the old Adamic nature would not simply yield to this new spiritual life, even in a redeemed individual. The old nature would be in conflict with the new nature in him, always contesting each other for supremacy. Had this not been evident in the lives of the disciples? Although they had given up their livelihoods and followed Jesus; although they had been taught by Him and lived closely with Him for three years; although they loved Jesus and had seen proof that He was indeed the Christ; although He modelled for them the love of God, the disciples remained dominated by their emotions and self-will . . . earthbound. A deeper, more fundamental change had to occur. If they were to survive and fulfill the commission with which they had been entrusted, something more was required.

> **" The Holy Spirit is fully God and He loves
> us with the same pure and intense
> love of the Father and the Son. "**

God's extraordinary plan was to now come to man in the person of the Holy Spirit who Jesus referred to as 'the Comforter.' The Holy Spirit is God's Spirit—the attributes and power of God: His faculty, His wisdom and His energy. He is the third person of the Trinity Who co-existed with God the Father and the Word from the beginning. Thus, He is called the "Eternal Spirit" (Hebrews 9:14). It was through His consummate power that the worlds were created in perfect precision, as the Father willed it and the Word spoke it (Genesis 1:2). He is the One Who overshadowed Mary and caused her to conceive without human intervention. He is the Spirit of Truth (John 16:13) and the One Who anointed Jesus with supernatural power, wisdom and knowledge to accomplish His mission while clothed in the flesh (Luke 4:18). He is the One by Whose power Jesus was raised from the dead (Romans 8:11). He is fully God and He loves us with the same pure and intense love of the Father and the Son.

This was the dispensation of the Holy Spirit, the third and final dispensation in God's plan to restore mankind to intimate relationship with the Trinity. Man would now also begin to learn who he was created to be—a son of God—and to cherish and operate in his spiritual birthright. God Himself, in the Person of the Holy Spirit would now come to dwell *within* the heart of the Christian. He would not have a physical body and would not relate to men through their senses but through their spirit. His mission would be to sensitize and develop their spirit through His influence and take them through the transition from operating in the sense realm to operating in the spirit realm, as it had been in the beginning. He would restore the Spirit to spirit dimension that was lost through Adam's fall.

The ushering in of the Holy Spirit is recorded by Luke, a physician in Jesus' day, who became a close follower and disciple of Jesus Christ. After the ascension of Jesus, Luke, under the influence of the Holy Spirit, wrote an expository on the life of Jesus to his friend, Theophilus, giving him an eyewitness account of Jesus' ministry. He expounds on His last moments on the earth and includes Jesus' promise to send the Holy Spirit in His stead, through Whom the work of restoring man's relationship with God would be accomplished. This promise is not just to the disciples, but is extended to all believers in Jesus Christ. In his account, Luke relives, for Theophilus and for us, what actually took place upon the entrance of the Holy Spirit.

> The former treatise have I made, O Theophilus, of all that
> Jesus began both to do and teach,[2] Until the day in which he
> was taken up, after that he through the Holy Ghost had given

commandments unto the apostles whom he had chosen:[3] To whom also he shewed himself alive after his passion by many infallible proofs, being seen of them forty days, and speaking of the things pertaining to the kingdom of God:[4] And, being assembled together with them, commanded them that they should not depart from Jerusalem, but wait for the promise of the Father, which, saith he, ye have heard of me.[5] For John truly baptized with water; but ye shall be baptized with the Holy Ghost not many days hence.[6] When they therefore were come together, they asked of him, saying, Lord, wilt thou at this time restore again the kingdom to Israel?[7] And he said unto them, It is not for you to know the times or the seasons, which the Father hath put in his own power.[8] But ye shall receive power, after that the Holy Ghost is come upon you: and ye shall be witnesses unto me both in Jerusalem, and in all Judaea, and in Samaria, and unto the uttermost part of the earth.[9] And when he had spoken these things, while they beheld, he was taken up; and a cloud received him out of their sight.

—Acts 1:1–9

As the disciples longingly gazed toward heaven after Jesus was taken up, two angels appeared to them and reminded them of Jesus' promise to return.

And while they looked stedfastly toward heaven as he went up, behold, two men stood by them in white apparel;[11] Which also said, Ye men of Galilee, why stand ye gazing up into heaven? this same Jesus, which is taken up from you into heaven, shall so come in like manner as ye have seen him go into heaven.

—Acts 1:10–11

Not quite understanding, but in obedience to Jesus, the disciples went to Jerusalem as He had earlier instructed. There they remained steadfast in prayer and supplication:

Then returned they unto Jerusalem from the mount called Olivet, which is from Jerusalem a sabbath day's journey.[13] And when they were come in, they went up into an upper room, where abode both Peter, and James, and John, and Andrew, Philip, and Thomas, Bartholomew, and Matthew, James the son of Alphaeus, and Simon Zelotes, and Judas the brother of James.[14] These all continued with one accord in prayer and supplication, with the women, and Mary the mother of Jesus, and with his brethren.

—Acts 1:12–14

Finally, the much anticipated day arrived as the Holy Spirit made His entrance.

And when the day of Pentecost was fully come, they were all with one accord in one place.[2] And suddenly there came a sound from heaven as of a rushing mighty wind, and it filled all the house where they were sitting.[3] And there appeared unto them cloven tongues like as of fire, and it sat upon each of them.[4] And they were all filled with the Holy Ghost, and began to speak with other tongues, as the Spirit gave them utterance. [5] And there were dwelling at Jerusalem Jews, devout men, out of every nation under heaven.[6] Now when this was noised abroad, the multitude came together, and were confounded, because that every man heard them speak in his own language.[7] And they were all amazed and marvelled, saying one to another, Behold, are not all these which speak Galileans?[8] And how hear we every man in our own tongue, wherein we were born?[9] Parthians, and Medes, and Elamites, and the dwellers in Mesopotamia, and in Judaea, and Cappadocia, in Pontus, and Asia,[10] Phrygia, and Pamphylia, in Egypt, and in the parts of Libya about Cyrene, and strangers of Rome, Jews and proselytes,[11] Cretes and Arabians, we do hear them speak in our tongues the wonderful works of God.[12] And they were all amazed, and were in doubt, saying one to another, What meaneth this?[13] Others mocking said, These men are full of new wine.

—Acts 2:1–13

Listen now to Peter who boldly lifted up his voice and spoke out in response to the skeptics' queries, providing them with the revelation of what had taken place:

[14] But Peter, standing up with the eleven, lifted up his voice, and said unto them, Ye men of Judaea, and all ye that dwell at Jerusalem, be this known unto you, and hearken to my words:[15] For these are not drunken, as ye suppose, seeing it is but the third hour of the day.[16] But this is that which was spoken by the prophet Joel;[17] And it shall come to pass in the last days, saith God, I will pour out of my Spirit upon all flesh: and your sons and your daughters shall prophesy, and your young men shall see visions, and your old men shall dream dreams:[18] And on my servants and on my handmaidens I will pour out in those days of my Spirit; and they shall prophesy:[19] And I will shew wonders in heaven above, and signs in the earth beneath; blood, and fire, and vapour of smoke:[20] The sun shall be turned into darkness, and the moon into blood, before that great and notable day of the Lord come:[21] And it shall come to pass, that whosoever shall call on the name of the Lord shall be saved.[22] Ye men of Israel, hear these words; Jesus of Nazareth, a man approved of God among you by miracles and wonders and signs, which God did by him in the midst of you, as ye yourselves also know:[23] Him, being delivered by the determinate counsel and foreknowledge of God, ye have taken, and by wicked hands have crucified and slain:[24] Whom God hath raised up, having loosed the pains of de

—Acts 2:14–24

Could this be the same man who had cowered in fear for his life and who had so emphatically denied even knowing Jesus? Where had these convicting words come from? How was it that he so readily quoted the words of the prophets of old? He was an unlearned man, a simple fisherman. He addressed the very ones who had killed Jesus and he boldly told them that they had done so "by their wicked hands"! From where did such authority and courage emanate? It was as if Peter and the other disciples had been transformed into completely new men! What had happened?

The Holy Spirit had come! He had come to *abide in them* forever just as Jesus had promised (John 14:16). He came on the day which in the Word of God is called, 'The Day of Pentecost'. Pentecost is the uniting of the believers in Jesus Christ and baptizing them—immersing their re-born spirit in Him—to form the spiritual 'Body of Christ', also called 'The Church of Jesus Christ'. It is a spiritual organism of which Jesus Christ is the Head.

Pentecost had ushered in this new dispensation—the dispensation of God the Holy Spirit. His mission was to represent God, His Word, His will and His plan through the life of the disciples and all who would accept Jesus Christ as their Saviour and Lord. Since the Holy Spirit is God in His fullness, the image and likeness of God is restored in the spirit of the believer when the Holy Spirit comes to live in his spirit. It is He who would bring the disciples and believers in Christ to full spiritual maturity.

Jesus had told the disciples that they would receive power when the Holy Spirit comes and that they would be His witnesses in Jerusalem, Judea, Samaria and even to the remote parts of the earth (Acts 1: 8).

The effect of that indwelling power of the Holy Spirit was immediately evident in the disciples. Peter, along with the other disciples who had waited in the upper room in obedience to Jesus' command had been baptized with the Holy Spirit. Their newborn spirits were filled with the Holy Spirit and immersed in the dynamic power of God. The fire of God fell on them, burning up the chaff, the self-life, the fleshly ambitions and behaviours. These ordinary, unsure, fickle and fearful men were now supernaturally converted into faithful, courageous disciples filled with the wisdom, knowledge and revelation of God and of His kingdom. They began to experience life in the spiritual dimension—no longer earthbound, but partaking of the divine nature of God as they focused solely on their Lord, Jesus Christ. Consumed with love and passion for Him and led by the Spirit of God, their fellowship, dialogue and Spirit-to-spirit intimacy with the Trinity continuously intensified. The baptism of fire by the Holy Spirit had so converted the disciples that they were now intimately joined with Jesus Christ and His purposes and they launched into the commission given by Him. In spite of the ever present threat of persecution before them, they boldly proclaimed the gospel of Jesus Christ with supernatural healings, miracles and signs.

The coming of the Holy Spirit to dwell in those whose spirit had been supernaturally regenerated at the 'new birth' experience is vital to the life of the believers in Jesus Christ and to the Church. Jesus Christ is the Head of His Church, which is a living, supernatural organism, made up of believers in Jesus Christ and it cannot be sustained without the indwelling of the Holy Spirit, the infilling of Spirit of God and the baptism of fire that the disciples experienced and which converted them. The Church of Jesus Christ did not come into existence by the ingenuity of man; it came into existence by the wisdom and power of God and is therefore supernaturally endowed. Without the Spirit of God, the Church would not be able to overcome the evils and deceptions which are in the world and which would try to destroy it. God had not left His Church powerless.

Indeed, the Holy Spirit gave supernatural gifts to the believers so that the Church of Jesus Christ would be established and sustained: Gifts of Revelation, Power and Inspiration. These gifts were to empower the disciples to preach the gospel, to bear witness of the truth of the gospel by signs and miracles and to strengthen the Church and keep them on the path that Jesus had ordained. On the day of Pentecost, as the disciples were baptized in the Holy Spirit and in fire, they spoke, by the power of the Holy Spirit, languages which they did not learn. This was an example of the Gift of Inspiration which is expressed vocally, through prophecy and through supernatural languages and the interpretations of these languages, which are referred to in the Word of God as "tongues". The impartation of this gift was yet another demonstration of the wisdom of God as men from many foreign nations and regions were present on that day and each heard the disciples proclaiming the mighty deeds of God in his own language. Many received the word preached and gave their hearts to Jesus Christ.

It was also through this gift of inspiration that the gospel of Jesus Christ and the epistles were written, as the Holy Spirit gave to the apostles the words by which all believers would be taught, nourished and sustained.

As these gifts began to operate, the Holy Spirit authenticated the preaching of the disciples as they declared the gospel of Jesus Christ. They performed healings and worked miracles which were demonstrations of the Gift of Power operating through them by the Holy Spirit. The Lord added to the Church radically, for truly the disciples had become His witnesses just as He had promised. Untold thousands of people responded to their testimony and became believers in Jesus Christ, brought to conviction of their sin by the power of the Holy Spirit.

" The Holy Spirit, the Spirit of Truth, is ever present with those who walk in truth and aspire to advance the Kingdom of God. "

Everyone who knew the disciples before recognized the change in their demeanour, their speech and their lifestyle. They spoke and operated more like Jesus as the Holy Spirit brought to their remembrance the words of Jesus Christ and gave them spiritual insight and understanding of His teachings. Their spirits began to mature as they lived by His Word and His principles. It was through this eternal Spirit of God that they now began to live in the supernatural (above the natural) dimension and to have fellowship with God . . . Spirit to spirit.

Believers are given these gifts of the Holy Spirit which enable them to transcend natural boundaries to work the works of God and to advance the

Kingdom of God in the manner in which Jesus Christ established it. It is through the gifts of the Holy Spirit that men appointed by Jesus Christ are able to fulfil the mandate of these offices and carry out the government of the Kingdom of God through the Church.

> Now there are diversities of gifts, but the same Spirit. [5] And there are differences of administrations, but the same Lord. [6] And there are diversities of operations, but it is the same God which worketh all in all. [7] But the manifestation of the Spirit is given to every man to profit withal.[8] For to one is given by the Spirit the word of wisdom; to another the word of knowledge by the same Spirit; [9] To another faith by the same Spirit; to another the gifts of healing by the same Spirit; [10] To another the working of miracles; to another prophecy; to another discerning of spirits; to another divers kinds of tongues; to another the interpretation of tongues: [11] But all these worketh that one and the selfsame Spirit, dividing to every man severally as he will. [12] For as the body is one, and hath many members, and all the members of that one body, being many, are one body: so also is Christ. [13] For by one Spirit are we all baptized into one body, whether we be Jews or Gentiles, whether we be bond or free; and have been all made to drink into one Spirit. [14] For the body is not one member, but many.
>
> —1 Corinthians 12:4–14

The Holy Spirit was given to the believers to encourage, exhort, edify and strengthen them in their faith, love and obedience to Jesus Christ and His word. He is ever present with those who are walking in truth and aspiring to advance the cause of Christ and the Kingdom of God. He is the Spirit of Truth and therefore withdraws from those who are in error and even from those who may have started in truth. He oversees the building of the Church, on Christ's behalf, working through the Christians whom He indwells. This is evident in the Book of Acts and in all the epistles written by the apostles, under His inspiration. The Holy Spirit was and is the driving force in those who stand firm in carrying the work of God forward at all cost. He is the One who preserves the faithful remnant of true believers through whom Jesus Christ would work to accomplish God's last upcoming move on the earth.

The Trinity's spiritual timetable is always precise. In this third dispensation, the Holy Spirit is here to bring to a conclusion, the work which God accomplished in the first dispensation and that which Jesus Christ accomplished in the second. His consummating mission in this, the maturity of times, is to prepare and position the faithful believers and followers of Jesus Christ for Christ's return to earth, which was promised by the angels at His ascension. He is raising up a spiritual army of the faithful who He will anoint with supernatural giftings of power that would be far greater than that which was seen in the early Church. This army will comprise mature sons of God whose lives are being directed solely by the Holy Spirit and through whom He would work the magnificent works of God and usher in that glorious climax of the ages. If you would be part of this end-time army it would be wise for you to yield to the leading of the Holy Spirit.

I shared these insights into the mystery of the Trinity out of my deep concern and longing to see all Christians become so intimately acquainted with the Trinity that they remain firmly rooted and grounded in the faith to which they belong. It is fitting therefore, that I end by making an earnest exhortation to you as the Apostle Paul did to the Church at Colossae:

> Beware lest any man spoil you through philosophy and vain deceit, after the tradition of men, after the rudiments of the world, and not after Christ. [9] For in him dwelleth all the fulness of the Godhead bodily. [10] And ye are complete in him, which is the head of all principality and power:
>
> —Colossians 2:8-10

EPILOGUE

These insights into the mystery of the Trinity reveal God's divine plan in the recovery and restoration of His children unto Him. Before man was placed on the earth, the Trinity had the knowledge that the day would come when Adam, the first man, would be disconnected from relationship, fellowship and dialogue with God. At that time each of the three Persons of the Trinity would manifest Himself, firstly, as Jehovah, the all-consuming, fearsome God; then as Jesus, The Word in flesh; and finally, as the Holy Spirit, God's Spirit. Together they would administer a plan of redemption and total restoration whereby man would be fully reunited with God.

This plan of God is on such a level of divine order that man, in his natural state, would not be able to comprehend it until God determines the time to unveil this mystery to the Church and the world. Now is that time.

In each dispensation, the Trinity was involved, but the contributing Person at each point in time was dominant while the other two Persons gave silent support.

God's love for mankind is so complete that He gave His entire being— His attributes and faculties expressed as three personalities: Father, Son and Holy Spirit—to restore man back to Himself, as it was with Adam before he sinned and fell. God condescended and took upon Himself the form of sinful man, gave Himself as the Sacrificial Lamb, paid the penalty for man's sin and took away the sin nature. Thus, God's justice was upheld and redeemed man was legally brought back into relationship, fellowship, and dialogue with Him.

No greater love story can ever be expressed and displayed, and no greater price can ever be paid. Christ paid a price that we cannot pay; a debt He did not owe.

The whole process of the Trinity's plan of redemption could have taken only a moment, but God's wisdom and perfection takes into account all of creation's responses to His methods and His manner of justice. God has revealed Himself as such a loving, merciful, and forgiving God that man's reasonable response to God would be to love Him with all our heart, mind and ability, and to live for Him, fulfilling the destiny He has allotted to us. Those who do, regain the honorable and glorious status: *Child of God–Son of God–Beloved of God.*

Author's Contact Information

Apostolic Renewal Ministries
Phone: (868) 637 5221 or Direct: (868) 632 1404
Email: arm@arm-tcc.org
Website: www.arm-tcc.org

Trinidad Christian Center
Phone: (868) 637 5221 or (868) 633 4037
Email: tcc@tcc1980.org
Website: www.tcc1980.org

CPSIA information can be obtained
at www.ICGtesting.com
Printed in the USA
LVOW04s1752080117
520188LV00014B/1387/P